REFLECTIONS
ON
REVIVAL
BY CHARLES G. FINNEY

Compiled by Donald W. Dayton

Bethany Fellowship INC.
MINNEAPOLIS, MINNESOTA 55438

Published by Bethany Fellowship, Inc.
6820 Auto Club Road, Minneapolis, Minnesota 55438

Printed in the United States of America

Library of Congress Cataloging in Publication Data

Finney, Charles Grandison, 1792-1875.
    Reflections on revival.

    First published in 1845 under title: Letters on revivals.
    1. Revivals—Addresses, essays, lectures. I. Dayton, Donald W.
II. Title.
BV3790.F514   1978   269'.2   78-26527
ISBN 0-87123-157-3

Foreword

Charles Grandison Finney (1792-1875) must "be reckoned among our great men," to use the words of American historian Richard Hofstadter. He was the most outstanding evangelist of the early nineteenth century, the heyday of Evangelicalism in America. But he was also an author, a professor of theology and a college president.

Finney has often been called the "Father of Modern Revivalism" because of his role in popularizing such practices as the "altar call" (or the "mourner's bench" that was used in his time), the "revival meeting" (the "protracted meeting" as they called it then), the special "inquirer's meeting," the use of extemporaneous preaching, and other "new measures" that have since become commonplace. He is probably best known for his *Lectures on Revivals of Religion* that were taken down stenographically as he delivered them weekly in 1835 to his New York congregation in the Chatham Street Chapel. These lectures have guided generations of Christians and evangelists seeking revival in their churches. Today, almost a century and a half later, they are still studied and treasured. Even those who do not share Finney's faith study this work to understand the development of American church life and culture.

But few of his readers today are aware of the fact that Finney also wrote another book on "revivals of religion," a series of "letters on revivals" first published in *The Oberlin Evangelist* from January 29, 1845, to June 24, 1846. These letters contain Finney's mature "reflections on revival." They were designed to correct some of his own earlier emphases and attempted to counteract both the resistance to revivals that dominated some quarters and the extremes that had developed in others. They also sought to deal with the problem of "backsliders" by calling converts to further spiritual growth and a "higher Christian life."

These letters reveal a Finney that breaks through the caricatures and stereotypes by which he has been maligned by both Christians and non-Christians. We find Finney recognizing the value of emotion in religious life, but also affirming the role of the mind and rational reflection. We see Finney, the evangelist, warning his fellow evangelists not to destroy the "pastoral relation" and calling them to support the church and the ongoing spiritual feeding of converts.

Finney turns out to be an evangelist with a burning social passion, arguing that the spiritual vitality of the church is sapped not by her involvement in social reform but by her avoidance of such issues. And we find a humble Finney to confess his own mistakes and admit, for example, that in earlier years he had placed too much emphasis on the "natural ability" of sinners to respond to God and not enough on the power of the grace of God to change the human heart.

These "letters on revivals" were published in book form both here and in Britain during the nineteenth century. But recent editions, under the title *Revival Fire*, have unwittingly been based on heavily abridged versions that distorted Finney's position, obscuring, for example, his commitment to social reform, his concern for the normal life of the church, and his awareness of some of the dangers of revivalism. Almost two decades ago William G. McLoughlin, editor of the Harvard University Press edition of *The Lectures on Revivals of Religion*, suggested that "some publisher will render a service to evangelical and historical literature by resurrecting these pithy, personal comments on revivalism by the nineteenth century's foremost evangelist." Bethany Fellowship has taken up that challenge and now provides, for the first time in over a century, the full collection of letters entitled *Reflections on Revival*.

Donald W. Dayton
North Park Theological Seminary

Introduction

Prof. Finney's Letters on Revivals

We commence this series, expecting it to be continued till it is closed. We have no doubt they will be read with deep interest and rich profit. Will our readers take special pains that these letters be read by all ministers of every denomination who pray for revivals, and by all lay brethren too who labor and pray for these seasons of refreshing from the presence of the Lord?

One word as to the value of Prof. Finney's experience for the past ten years. During my own labors as a pastor, I attended some scores of protracted meetings, often in connection with evangelists. I watched the results of these meetings for months and years after they had passed, and plainly saw in the manifest bearings which the mode of conducting these meetings had upon the future prosperity of the church, that every evangelist ought to follow his revivals into their decline, and study the causes of this decline, before he could be fitted to do evangelistic work in the most skillful way. More than once have I said to evangelists, "Come, let us go, like Paul and Barnabas, and visit the churches where you labored, and see how they do. I have so strong a conviction of the importance of this work, that I will cheerfully leave my parish for a while and go with you." No conviction can be stronger on my mind than this, that in this way only can we rationally expect to see the true philosophy of conducting revivals and protracted meetings ever thoroughly developed. We must learn to take into view not only present but remote results; not only the present excitement, but the remote fruits of stable, consistent, untiring piety.

Now Bro. Finney's situation for the past ten years has spread out before him precisely these fields of observation. No circumstances could be more favorable than his for watching the after developments and remote results of protracted efforts and revival measures. It need not be said that his eye penetrates the causes of spiritual results with uncommon sagacity. Few men have ever been more at home in the world of spiritual experience. We venture to express the belief that his views will commend themselves to the sober judgment of the great mass of those who have labored in revivals, and have studied faithfully their character and results.

—Oberlin Evangelist, 1845

Contents

Chapter I

REVIVAL METHODS

Beloved in the Lord:

Many of you are aware that several years have passed since a series of lectures on the subject of revivals was published through the columns of the New York Evangelist. These lectures were preached by me to my own congregation in the city of New York, and reported by the editor of that paper. Since the publication of those lectures, my observation and experience on the subject have been continually developing and ripening until I am very desirous of saying many additional things to my brethren on this subject.

When I first began to preach, I was without knowledge and without experience on the subject of revivals. I had but a very limited Christian experience. The Lord led me in a way that I knew not. I have recently thought that it might be useful to the churches, to communicate to them my ripened experience and convictions upon the same subject. I can see that in some things I erred in manner and in spirit; which things I want to point out both by way of confessing my own faults, and as a warning to others. In many things also, I fell short of securing all the desirable results which might have been secured, had I been free from the faults to which I have alluded, and had I understood and applied all the necessary means and truths to bring forward and promote that ripeness of experience and growth in grace which is indispensable to prevent reaction and disasters following revivals.

It is no part of my design to wage a war of words or opinions with my brethren, nor indeed is controversy in form or spirit, any part of my object. It is not a difference of metaphysical or theological views between myself and my brethren, upon which I wish to insist. But the thing I desire is to be permitted to call their attention to certain facts and results with their causes, which it seems to me of the highest importance to the church well to consider.

I wish the brethren particularly to understand that I lay no claim to infallibility upon this subject. I only wish to give my opinions with that modesty which becomes my ignorance, and which is demanded also by the nature of the subject.

I have had a continual experience upon the subject of revivals of religion, now for about twenty years; in the course of which experience, I have watched narrowly and with much solicitude the various types, developments, results, and indeed all the phenomena pertaining to them, and resulting from them. I have occasionally seen remarks in some of the newspapers assuming that since my residence in Oberlin, I have ceased to witness powerful revivals of religion in connection with my labors and the labors of those connected with me; but this is a great mistake, as my brethren generally would have been informed had not some of the leading papers which have made the assumption just mentioned, declined giving to the public the facts as they are and have been. I do not mention this either to censure those editors, or to boast of the success of my own labors and of those associated with me, but simply to bespeak your unbiased attention to what I have to say as coming not from one whose observation and experience in revivals have long ago ceased, but from one whose opportunities for observation and experience have continued in their freshness up to the present hour. Since I have been here, my position at home and my observation abroad have given me peculiar advantages for judging of the expediency and inexpediency of certain measures. I have seen powerful revivals in this place from time to time now for about ten years, and indeed the state of things has generally been such here as would elsewhere have been considered a revival state. Scarcely a week or even a day has passed without more or less cases coming under my observation of manifest divine influence. I have had an opportunity to witness the results of revivals in their influence over young men preparing for the ministry, over ministers themselves, over the community at large, and for years after their occurrence. I have marked with the deepest interest their rise, their progress, their temporary decline, and again their revival, the various types they have taken on, and the occasion of these modifications together with what I deem to be disastrous, dangerous, useful.

There is a considerable number of topics to which I desire to call the attention of my brethren. In the providence of God, I have witnessed a great variety of methods in conducting revivals. When I first began to be acquainted with them, and for about ten years of my earliest labors, what are now termed protracted meetings were not known; since which, these meetings first styled 'conferences of churches,' then 'three days' meetings,' then 'four days' meetings,' and subsequently 'protracted meetings,' extending continuously through several weeks, have been the order of the day. In respect to the expediency as manifested in the results of these different methods, I have several things to say, to which I invite the prayerful consideration of all classes of Christians. Also with respect to the great care that should be taken to prevent their degenerating into a spirit of fanaticism and misrule, as in at least some instances they manifestly have done. I wish also to call the attention of the brethren to the occasions of those disastrous results. Also to the great importance of stated or settled pastors to watch over, carry out, and secure the desirable results of revivals, and the almost certainly disastrous consequences of disturbing the pastoral relation. I have also many things to say on the subject of cultivating high spirituality in converts, and securing them against those declensions which have so disgraced revivals. I cannot pretend at this time to enumerate the topics on which I wish to write, but would only at present bespeak the attention of my brethren to the series of short letters which I intend to address to them. I have another series in contemplation, upon the subject of the controversies, and the controversial spirit of the present day, which I hope to lay before my brethren at no distant period, should the Lord spare my life and give me opportunity.

Your brother,

C. G. Finney

February 12, 1845

Dear Brethren:

I have observed, and multitudes of others also I find have observed, that for the last ten years, revivals of religion have been gradually becoming more and more superficial. All the phenomena which they exhibit testify to this as a general fact. There is very much less deep conviction of sin and deep breaking up of the heart; much less depth of humility and much less strength in all the graces exhibited by converts in late revivals, than in the converts from the revivals which occurred about 1830 and 1831 and for some time previous. I have observed, as have others also, that revivals are of much shorter duration, and that a reaction comes on much more suddenly and disastrously than formerly. Also that fewer of the converts make stable and efficient Christians; that those who do persevere, appear to much less advantage, and exhibit, as a general thing, much less of the Spirit of Christ than in former revivals; have not so much of the spirit of prayer, and are not so modest and humble. In short, all the phenomena of the more recent revivals, judging from my own experience and observation and from the testimony of other witnesses, show that they have, at least very extensively, taken on a much less desirable type than formerly. Christians are much less spiritual in revivals, much less prevalent in prayer, not so deeply humbled and quickened and thoroughly baptized with the Holy Ghost as they were formerly. These statements I do not suppose to be universally applicable to modern revivals, but I do believe them to be applicable generally. As revivals now exist, I believe ministers are not nearly as desirous of seeing them in their congregations as they formerly were, nor have they good reason to be. Those ministers who have witnessed none but the later revivals of which I speak, are almost afraid of revivals. They have seen the disastrous results of modern revivals so frequently, that they honestly entertain the doubt whether they are upon the whole desirable. Those, as I have good reason to know, who saw the revivals which occurred ten or twenty years ago, greatly prefer revivals of that type. They are distressed with the superficiality of many recent revivals. I make this as a general, not a universal remark, and state only my own opinion of public sentiment. I have often heard it said both among ministers and private Christians, we long to see the days return when we shall have such revivals as we saw years ago. I have been anxiously watching the progress of things in this direction, and enquiring as carefully and prayerfully as I could into the causes which are operating to produce these results. If I am not misinformed, and have not greatly misapprehended the case, the following will be found among them:

1. There is much less probing of the heart by a deep

and thorough exhibition of human depravity, than was formerly the case. It has been of late a common remark, and a brother who has long labored as an evangelist made the same remark, that for the last few years there has been little or no opposition made by impenitent sinners to revivals. Now it is not because the carnal mind is not still enmity against God, but I greatly fear it is for the want of thoroughly turning up to the light the deep foundations of this enmity in their hearts. The unutterable depravity of the human heart has not, I fear, been laid open to the very bottom as it formerly was. A few sermons on the subject of moral depravity are generally preached in every revival, but I fear this is by no means the great theme of the preaching so much and so long as it ought to be, in order thoroughly to break up the fallow ground of the sinner's and the professor's heart. From my own experience and observation, as well as from the word of God, I am fully convinced that the character of revivals depends very much upon the stress that is laid upon the depravity of the heart. Its pride, enmity, windings, deceitfulness, and everything else that is hateful to God should be exposed in the light of his perfect law.

2. I fear that stress enough is not laid upon the horrible guilt of this depravity. Pains enough is not taken by a series of pointed and cutting discourses, to show the sinner the utter inexcusableness, the unutterable wickedness and guilt of his base heart. No revival can be thorough until sinners and backsliders are so searched and humbled that they cannot hold up their heads. It is a settled point with me, that while backsliders and sinners can come to an anxious meeting and hold up their heads and look you and others in the face without blushing and confusion, the work of searching is by no means performed, and they are in no state to be thoroughly broken down and converted to God. I wish to call the attention of my brethren especially to this fact.

When sinners and backsliders are really convicted by the Holy Ghost, they are greatly ashamed of themselves. Until they manifest deep shame, it should be known that the probe is not used sufficiently, and they do not see themselves as they ought. When I go into a meeting of inquiry and look over the multitudes, if I see them with heads up, looking at me and at each other, I have learned to understand what work I have to do. Instead of pressing them immediately to come to Christ, I must go to work to convict them of sin. Generally by looking over the room, a minister can easily tell, not only who are convicted and who are not, but who are so deeply convicted as to be prepared to receive Christ. Some are looking around and manifest no shame at all; others cannot look you in the face and yet can hold up their heads; others still cannot hold up their heads and yet are silent; others by their sobbing, and breathing, and agonizing, reveal at once the fact that the sword of the Spirit has wounded them to their very heart. Now I have learned that a revival never does take on a desirable and wholesome type any farther than the preaching and means are so directed, and so efficient as to produce that kind of genuine and deep conviction which breaks the sinner and the backslider right down, and makes him unutterably ashamed and confounded before the Lord until he is not only stripped of every excuse, but driven to go all lengths in justifying God and condemning himself.

3. I have thought that at least in a great many instances, stress enough has not been laid upon the necessity of divine influence upon the hearts of Christians and of sinners. I am confident that I have sometimes erred in this respect myself. In order to rout sinners and backsliders from their self-justifying pleas and refuges, I have laid, and I doubt not that others also have laid too much stress upon the natural ability of sinners to the neglect of showing them the nature and extent of their dependence upon the grace of God and the

influence of his Spirit. This has grieved the Spirit of God. His work not being honored by being made sufficiently prominent, and not being able to get the glory to himself of his own work, he has withheld his influences. In the meantime multitudes have been greatly excited by the means used to promote an excitement, and have obtained hopes, without ever knowing the necessity of the presence and powerful agency of the Holy Ghost. It hardly need be said that such hopes are better thrown away than kept. It were strange indeed if one could lead a Christian life upon the foundation of an experience in which the Holy Ghost is not recognized as having any thing to do.

Your brother,

C. G. Finney

February 26, 1845

Dear Brethren:

I have already intimated that pains enough had not been taken to search the heart and thoroughly detect and expose the sinner's depravity, so as to make him see the need of the gospel remedy. If I am not mistaken there has been in many cases an error committed in urging sinners to submission before they are prepared to understand what true submission is. They have been urged to repent before they have really understood the nature and desert of sin; to believe before they have understood their need of Christ; to resolve to serve God before they have at all understood what the service of God is. They have been pressed to make up their minds to enter immediately upon the service of God, and have been taught that they needed only to make a resolution to obey the Lord. Hence their religion, after all, has been only a religion of resolutions, instead of a religion of faith, and love, and of a broken heart. In short it appears to me, that in many instances the true idea of what constitutes pure religion has not been developed in the mind, and that consequently spurious conversions have been distressingly numerous. I have been more and more surprised from year to year to find how very numerous those professors of religion are, who manifestly have not the true ideal of pure religion before their minds. It seems that in many instances the idea that love is the essence and the whole of religion, is left almost, if not entirely out of view.

There seem to be two extremes towards which different classes of persons have been continually verging. These extremes are Antinomianism on the one hand, and legality on the other—both manifestly at an equal remove from the true idea of religion.

The religion of the legalist is one of resolutions. He resolves to serve the Lord. He makes up his mind, as he says. He gets the idea that to serve the Lord is to go to work—to pray in his family—to attend meetings—to visit, and talk, and bustle about, and do the work of the Lord, as he calls it—and this with a perfectly legal spirit, with none of that love, gentleness, meekness, long-suffering, and those fruits of the Spirit which characterize true Christianity. He easily works himself into an excitement, but after all, has not the root of the matter in him, and makes out to keep up what he calls his working for God only during a protracted meeting. Probably three months of the year is the utmost extent of his piety; in many instances probably, it does not amount to even half that. Now the difficulty in this case is, that the individual has not the root of the matter in him. The fountain of the great deep of selfishness has not been broken up. He has never been thoroughly convicted of sin by the Holy Ghost. His convictions of sin have been little more than those natural and necessary affirmations of his own mind under a clear exhibition of truth by the preacher without any supernatural illumination by the Spirit of God. Consequently all his ideas of God, of sin, of his own guilt and desert of punishment, his need of a Savior, the necessity of his being saved from his sins—in short, every fundamental idea of the Christian religion is apprehended by him with very little clearness. His mind is dark; his heart is hard. He has never been stripped of his self-dependence and self-righteousness; consequently, he has never known Christ, "the power of his resurrection, the fellowship of his sufferings," nor the "being made conformable to his death"; nor has he even an idea of what these things mean. He knows little of Christ more than the name, and an obscure idea of his mediatorial work and relations. He has never been slain by the law, and found himself a dead, condemned, and lost sinner; and consequently, dead to all tendency towards God. He has no deep consciousness of sustaining the relation of an outlaw and a condemned criminal to the government of God, and being dead to all hope in himself or in any other creature. In short, instead of seeing his necessities, his true character and relations, his views of all these things are so exceedingly superficial, that he has not apprehended and does not apprehend the necessity and nature of gospel salvation. He goes about, working for God just as he would serve a man for wages, and in the same sense. His religion is not that of disinterested and universal benevolence; but he makes up his mind to serve God, just as he would make up his mind in any matter of barter, or to render a piece of service to anybody else, for value received or to be received.

This class of converts may generally be distinguished by the following, among other characteristics.

1. There is a manifest want of meekness, humility, and lowliness of mind in their religion. The fact is, they never have been humbled and broken down, and consequently they do not exhibit this state of mind. Their deportment, conversation, bearing, their prayers and exhortations, all savor of a self-righteous spirit.

2. There is a manifest want of love in their religion; in other words, their religion is not love. The manner in which they speak of old professors of religion, of Christians and ministers, and indeed of all classes, demonstrates that the law of kindness and love is not in their hearts, and consequently is not on their tongues. They are not tender of the reputation of others, regardless of their feelings, alive to their interests, gentle, kind, and courteous as those that are actuated by love. Observe them, and you will see that their religion wants the attributes laid down by Paul in 1 Cor. 13. It has not that charity which suffereth long and is kind, which envieth not, vaunteth not itself, is not puffed up, doth not behave itself unseemly, which thinketh no evil, rejoiceth not in iniquity, but rejoiceth in the truth. This religion, which beareth, believeth, hopeth, endureth all, is not theirs.

3. Another obvious characteristic in this class of converts is, that there is very little of Christ in their religion. They will manifest in their conversation, prayers, and in many ways, that they have not been emptied of themselves and filled with Christ.

Another characteristic will be, they are not Bible students. They do not after all, relish and deeply search the Bible. The fact is, they understand it but very slightly. They have not been so subdued that the language of the inspired writers is the natural language of their own experience. This is the secret of their not understanding, loving, and searching it. No person really understands and loves his Bible until he has such an experience as accords with the language of the Bible and no farther than his experience accords with the inspired writer's, does the Bible become intelligible and deeply interesting to him. Now I have observed that there are a great many professors who neither know nor care much about their Bibles. There are even some young preachers, or *professed* preachers, who know almost nothing about their Bibles, and who in fact read other things ten times as much as they read the Book of God. A vast number of professed converts know full well, and those who are well acquainted with them must also know, that they are but little interested in their Bibles. Now all this shows conclusively, that their religion is not Bible religion, that they are not "on the foundation of the apostles and prophets, Jesus Christ himself being the chief cornerstone."

Yours in Jesus,

C. G. Finney

March 12, 1845

Dear Brethren:

I said in my last letter that there seemed to be two extremes toward which different classes of persons are continually verging. Those extremes are Antinomianism on the one hand, and legality on the other—both manifestly at an equal removed from the true idea of religion. In that letter I made some remarks upon the class of legalists; in this I propose to notice the Antinomian class.

Antinomianism is the opposite extreme to legalism. Legalists are all work, and Antinomians no work. The

latter have almost universally been legalists and very
self-righteous. They have done a great deal of hard labor
in their own strength, and in a perfectly legal, as opposed to an evangelical spirit. They have depended on
their own resolutions, and have found them a bruised
reed and a broken staff. In short, they have generally
gone through nearly every stage of legal experience, from
the dead formality of a self-righteous Pharisee to the
sharp conflicts and agonizing efforts described in
Romans seven. They have known what it is to be blind to
their own sins, and also what it is to be in a good
measure awake to their sins; what it is to make almost
no effort to serve the Lord, and what it is to make most
agonizing efforts in their own strength. They have
generally been brought to see the futility, emptiness,
and downright wickedness of all these self-righteous,
self-originated, and self-sustained efforts. Finding their
own impotence, and being bad philosophers, they vault
quite over into the opposite extreme, and from being all
work and no faith, they become all faith and no work;
not considering that this kind of faith is dead, being
alone. They seem not aware that their faith is a state of
the sensibility and not of the heart; a passive and not an
active state of mind. It does not touch the will; if it did,
their works would show it.

That they come into this state usually, by swinging
like a pendulum from one extreme to the other, is most
manifest. Having learned the folly of self-righteous and
self-originated efforts, they feel a kind of contempt for all effort, and fall right back into a state of supineness and
quietism. Professing to have yielded up their whole agency
to Christ, they throw all the responsibility upon him and do
nothing. Under pretence of being led by the Spirit and of
waiting for God to reveal his will to them, they give themselves up very much to spiritual indolence.

This class of persons are extremely apt to suppose
that all efforts to promote revivals are of course legal ef-

forts, such as they are conscious they used to make. The active Christian who sympathizes with Christ and is led by the Spirit to labor as Christ and the Apostles labored, they look upon as being engaged as they formerly were, running before they are sent, going forward in their own strength, self-righteous and legal. Now these dear souls do not realize that there is such a thing as great spiritual activity and aggressiveness, and that true spirituality always implies this; that true faith always begets sympathy with Christ, that true Christianity is always and necessarily the spirit of missions, of revivals, of self-sacrifice, of holy activity; that is a living, energizing principle; that holiness in man is just what it was in Christ; indeed that holiness is always one and the same thing—benevolence or good-willing—and by a law of its own nature is continually putting forth efforts to realize the great end of benevolence; namely, the highest good of all beings. True Christianity is the law of love written in the heart by the Holy Spirit, and of course necessarily acted out in practical life. Now anything that professes to be Christianity and does not sympathize with Christ must be a delusion.

The mistake of the Antinomian lies not, as with the legalist, in the want of apprehending the emptiness, folly, and even wickedness of all self-righteous efforts to please God, but rather in a mistaken apprehension of the nature of faith and of true religion. They do not distinguish between that faith which consists in a persuasion of the intellect, accompanied by a corresponding state of feeling, in which however there is no assent of the heart or will; and that faith in which the heart or will most fully yields to perceived and admitted truth. The faith of the heart is necessarily a powerful and active principle. The faith of the intellect, or mere intellectual apprehension, accompanied with corresponding feelings, is not a voluntary, active, and energizing principle. This should always be understood. It is often not very easy to distinguish between these two. It should always be remembered, that where the faith of the heart or true faith exists, the other also does and must exist; that is, where the heart confides in the truth of God, there must be an intellectual apprehension of truth and a corresponding state of feeling, so that true faith cannot exist without the other, though the other may exist without it; that is, the intellect may apprehend the truth, the feelings may be affected by it, while the heart does not receive it.

There is another mistake into which Antinomians fall, of a very serious character. Indeed there are many, but one is of too much importance to be omitted here. I refer to their mistake in respect to being led by the Spirit of God. The manner in which they expect and profess to be led by the Spirit, seems to be that of impulse rather than divine illumination through the word. They sometimes seem to suppose that the Spirit leads the people of God by impressions upon their sensibility or feelings, rather than by enlightening their intelligence, and leading them to act rationally, and in accordance with the written word. This is undoubtedly a great and fundamental error. True religion does not consist in obeying our feelings, but in conforming our heart to the law of our intelligence. Mere feeling is blind; and to follow it is never virtue. Now for persons to give themselves up to follow mere impressions on their sensibility, is not to be led by the Spirit of God, but by the ever-varying fluctuations and effervescings of their own restless and agitated sensibility. There is no end to the mistakes into which souls may be led in this way. God has given us reason, and requires us to understand what we are about. He has given us the written word, and the Holy Spirit to shine upon it, to make us understand its great principles and the application of them to all the circumstances and duties of life. Surely then it is a great mistake to give ourselves up to blind impulse, instead of submitting ourselves to be taught and led of God in his plainly appointed way. Antinomians amuse themselves very much with views and consequent feelings. They often seem to be very happy in certain views which they have of Christ and of gospel salvation, while it cannot be perceived that they really sympathize with Christ in the great work of saving souls.

Now as I said in my last letter, this is one extreme, and legality is another extreme. The truth lies between them. A true Christian is active, but his activity and energy arise out of a deep sympathy with the indwelling Spirit of Christ. Christ is formed within him. The Spirit of Christ is the mighty energizing power of his soul. The law of the spirit of life in Christ Jesus has made him free from the law of sin and death. In short, he has become dead to the law. He may be as active as he ever was in the days of his most strenuous legality, and even more so. His strenuousness, energy and zeal are not at all abated, but generally increased. Indeed they are always increased, unless the comparison be made with his most convicted and agonized legal states. But his activity is that of love and faith. It is the activity of the eternal life of Christ that dwells within him. Now Antinomians commit a great mistake when they do not distinguish between this activity and their own former legal activity.

Again, I should say that legalists are exceedingly apt to reproach Antinomians without any very good reasons. In their bustle and zeal they seem to have the very spirit of Jehu. They drive furiously and seem to say—"Come see my zeal for the Lord." Now as a matter of fact, their legal bustle is not a whit better than Antinomian quietism. They would indeed compass sea and land to make one proselyte; but he is after all, a legalist like themselves; for they beget children in their own likeness.

Now it appears to me to be of the last importance that such discriminations should be made as to guard, if possible, against these two extremes, and so to conduct revivals of religion that the churches will take the middle ground; that is, that they will have the true idea of religion developed in their minds, and the true spirit of it in their hearts. So far as this can be secured, religious excitements are valuable and desirable, but no farther. It is very easy to show that there are many excitements that are not revivals of true religion; but this must be deferred to a future letter.

Your brother,

C. G. Finney

March 26, 1845

Dear Brethren:

Another error in the promotion of revivals is a want of such discrimination in the instructions given, as thoroughly to develop the true idea of religion in the mind. I have been astonished and greatly pained, to find how few professors of religion seem ever to have had the true idea of the Christian religion distinctly in their minds. Great multitudes suppose it to consist merely in certain feelings and emotions, and mere passive states of mind. Consequently when they speak of their religion, they speak of their feelings. I feel thus and so. They seem to suppose that religion consists almost if not altogether in certain states of the sensibility, in which strictly speaking there can be no religion at all.

Multitudes make their religion consist in desires as distinct from choice and action of the will, in which certainly there can be no religion, if we use the term desire as I now do, in the sense of a passive as opposed to a voluntary state of mind. Others have supposed religion to consist in a merely legal state, in which the mind is lashed up by conscience to a reluctant performance of what it calls duty. Indeed there is almost every form of error in respect to what really constitutes true religion. Men seem to have no just idea of the nature of sin or of holiness. Selfishness is often spoken of by many professors of religion as if it were hardly to be considered sinful, and if sinful at all, only one form of sin. When I have had occasion to preach in different places on the subject of selfishness, I have been surprised to find that great numbers of professors of religion have been struck with the idea as if it were new, that selfishness is entirely inconsistent with a religious state of mind. They seem never to have dreamed that all selfishness is inconsistent with religion. In preaching in one of our cities I was endeavoring to develop the true idea of the Christian religion and demonstrate that it consisted alone in love, or in disinterested, perfect and universal benevolence. The idea that religion consisted in benevolence seemed to be entirely new to great multitudes of professors of religion. And on one occasion when this subject had been presented and turned over and over until the congregation understood it, a deacon of one of the churches remarked to me as I came out of the pulpit that he did not believe there were ten real Christians in the city, and a lady said she did not know of but one person in the church to which she belonged who had the religion of benevolence. All the rest, so far as she knew them, appeared to be under the dominion of selfishness. If I am not mistaken, there certainly is a great want of just and thorough discrimination on this subject in most of the congregations in this land, and especially is this manifest in seasons of revival. This is the very time to bring out and press these discriminations until the true idea of religion stands out in full development. Unless this is done, almost endless mistakes will be fallen into by professed converts. In a future letter I may point out some of these mistakes in detail; but here suffice it to say that it must be of essential importance that persons should understand what religion is, and that it is all summed up in one word, *love*; and that every form of true religion is only a modification of love or disinterested benevolence; that whatever does not proceed from love is not virtue or true religion. The enquirers should be instructed that to be converted is to love God with all their hearts. To repent is to turn away from selfishness, and give their hearts to God; in short that the first and only thing which they are required to do is to love the Lord with all their hearts and their neighbor as themselves, and that until they do love, whatever else they do they are not religious, and no farther than they are actuated by supreme love to God and equal love to man are they truly religious in any case whatever. Too much pains cannot be taken to correct the errors into which men are constantly falling on this subject. But while it is of vital importance to make these distinctions, let it be forever remembered that these discriminations themselves will never convert men to true religion. And here is another error into which if I mistake not some have fallen. They have spent their whole strength in making these distinctions and showing the philosophical nature of faith, of benevolence, of repentance and of the different Christian graces. They have perhaps made just discriminations and urged them nobly and efficiently until they have really developed correct ideas in the mind, but they have fallen short after all of promoting true religion, on account of one fundamental defect. For instance, when they have made just discriminations, and developed the true idea of faith, they have stopped short and suffered the mind to please itself with the idea, while the heart does not go forth to the realization of the idea. In other words they have failed to present the objects of faith, and to hold them before the mind until the mind believes. They philosophized, perhaps correctly about the nature of faith, but they have not so forcibly arrayed before the mind the truths to be believed as to beget faith. They have made men understand what faith is, but have not succeeded in persuading them to exercise faith. They have been satisfied with developing the idea, without pressing the truth to be believed, and holding the objects of faith before the mind, until the will yields and commits itself to them in the exercise of faith. The same has been true of every other Christian grace. They have developed the true idea of benevolence, but have not pressed those considerations that tend to make the mind benevolent, until it has broken loose from its selfishness and wholly committed itself to the exercise of benevolence. It is certainly an important distinction which I have before my mind. A man may understand the philosophical nature of benevolence without being benevolent. If we satisfy ourselves with developing the true idea of benevolence and do not so present God, Christ, the love of Christ, the great interests of the universe, and all the moving considerations which tend to make the mind benevolent, although we may develop the true idea of religion, we may fail of securing true religion. Some as I have said have greatly erred in not making just discriminations in respect to the nature of true religion, and converts have taken up with something else, supposing it to be the religion of Christ. Others have made just discriminations until they have developed the idea, and converts have mistaken the idea of true religion as it lies developed in the intelligence for religion itself. Seeing what it is so clearly, they think they have it. They understand it and do not realize that they do not exercise it. Now both these things need to be thoroughly attended to, in order to secure sound conversions. Especially is this true since a false philosophy has engendered false ideas of religion in so many minds.

What is true of faith and love, is true of repentance, humility, meekness, and every grace. Not only should its philosophical nature be defined, until its true idea is developed in the intelligence, but those truths that tend to produce it should be pressed, and turned over and explained and held up before the mind, until the heart goes forth in the exercise of these virtues. Let it be understood that the philosophical explanations which develop the idea of these virtues have no tendency to beget them. It is only a lucid and forcible exhibition of appropriate truths, such as makes its appeal to the heart, that can ever be instrumental in begetting true religion. And here I would say that if either class of truths is to be omitted, the discriminations of which I have spoken can be omitted with the greatest safety, for if we hold forth the objects of faith and love, and strongly present and press these truths, they tend to beget repentance, faith, love, humility, meekness, etc. We may expect in multitudes of instances to beget these forms of virtue in their purity without the subject of them having an idea of their philosophical nature. By presenting Christ, for instance, a soul may be led to believe in him, without once thinking of the philosophical nature of true faith. By holding forth the character of God, true love may be begotten in the mind without the philosophical nature of love being at all understood by the mind, and this may be true of every grace, so that it is far better to hold forth those truths that tend to beget these graces, and omit the discriminations that would develop their philosophical ideal, than to make discriminations, and leave out of view, or slightly exhibit the truths that are indispensable to engage the obedience of the heart. The discriminations of which I have spoken that develop the true idea are mostly important to cut up the false hopes of old professors and spurious converts, and to prevent enquirers from falling into error. And I would beseech my brethren who are engaged in promoting revivals of religion, to remember and carry into practice this important consideration, that the gospel is to be set forth in all its burning and overcoming power, as the thing to be believed, until the Christian graces are brought into exercise, and that occasionally in the course of revival preaching, the preacher should bring forth these fundamental discriminations. They should develop the true idea of religion and prevent false hopes.

Your brother,

C. G. Finney

April 9, 1845

Dear Brethren:

Another error which has prevailed to some extent, I fear, in the promotion of revivals, has been a kind of preaching that has rather puffed up than humbled and subdued the mind. I mean a kind of preaching which dwells much more on the philosophy of religion than the great facts of revelation. Into this mistake I am sure that I have often fallen myself. Where the preaching is so metaphysical and philosophical, as to leave the impression that everything about religion can be comprehended, and that nothing can be received which cannot be explained, and its philosophy understood, great mischief is a certain result. I do not suppose that any have fallen into the error of declaring that nothing is to be received by faith that cannot be philosophically explained and understood, yet if I am not mistaken this impression has been left after all. The human mind is so desperately wicked, so self-complacent on the one hand, and so unbelieving on the other, that it is greatly flattered and puffed up when it indulges in metaphysical and philosophical speculations about the truths of religion until it fancies itself able to comprehend most or all of the great truths that relate to God and his kingdom.

Now two evils result directly from this course of instruction. First, it substitutes our own ratiocinations for faith. When men philosophize or speculate about a doctrine until they see it to be philosophical, they are exceedingly apt to rest in their own demonstrations or philosophical conclusions rather than in the testimony of God. But this is not faith. When men have formed this habit, they will either wholly reject all doctrines which they cannot philosophically comprehend and explain, or they will hold them so loosely that it can be easily seen they have no real confidence in them. Such men, so far as you can commend yourself to their intelligence, by explaining everything to their comprehension, will go along with you; but they manifestly go along under the influence of your speculations and reasonings, and not at all because they implicitly confide in the testimony of God in regard to the facts of the gospel. Now it will be found that this class of Christians either absolutely reject, or hold very loosely some of the most important and precious doctrines of the gospel, such as the divinity and humanity of Christ, the doctrine of the trinity, the divine purposes, and many other truths connected with these. This kind of preaching serves not to humble the pride of the human mind but conveys the very kind of knowledge which Paul says puffs up. I have often thought of that passage in witnessing the spirit of the class of converts to which I allude. They are manifestly wise in their own conceits. *They* understand what they believe. They pride themselves on being philosophers and in not ignorantly and weakly believing what they cannot understand. Now I have observed it to be perfectly manifest that this class of persons have no real faith. Their confidence is not at all in God, and the Bible, or in any of its statements, simply because God has declared them. They are pleased with and confide in their own speculations, and of course have but very little reverence for God, very little reverence for His authority, and no true confidence in His Word.

The evils of this kind of philosophical preaching are, first, it does not beget faith. Secondly, if faith once existed it has no tendency to develop, strengthen, and confirm it, but rather to wither and destroy it. It is a remarkable fact that the inspired writers never philosophize, but always *assume* a correct philosophy. They throw out facts on which faith may lay hold. Although they never philosophize, yet it will be seen that their method of presenting truth is truly philosophical, when we consider the end which they had in view. It is very plain that the scriptural method of presenting truth is the very one which of all others is calculated to secure the end which God has in view. Faith in the character and testimony of God is forever indispensable to heart-obedience to God in all worlds. Some talk about faith being swallowed up in vision in heaven; but this can never be. Confidence in God and His character, wisdom, goodness, and in the universality and perfection of His benevolence will no doubt be just as indispensable in heaven to all eternity as it is on earth. From the nature of the case it must be that very many of the divine dispensations in a government so vast, managed with a policy to us so inscrutable, must be deeply mysterious and perplexing to us unless we have the most implicit confidence in God's benevolence and wisdom. Now in this world the great object of God is to restore confidence in himself and his government; to beget and develop faith to the utmost. Consequently he presents facts without explaining them. He enters not at all into their philosophy, but simply asserts the facts which he desires to communicate, and leaves it for faith to lay hold upon and rest in them. Now many of these facts we can never comprehend. We may understand that a thing is true while we cannot explain its philosophy. This is no doubt true of myriads of facts which will be ever coming up in the administration of God's government. It is therefore indispensable that we should be trained in the very beginning of our Christian course to rest unhesitatingly in the facts and wait for the explanations until we are able to receive them. Too much stress therefore cannot be laid on so presenting the gospel as to give full scope for the exercise of faith. By this I do not mean that the facts are not to be explained if they admit of philosophical explanation, but I mean that too much pains should not be taken to explain and philosophize on facts lest by so doing you leave the impression that everything must be explained before it is received. In my own experience I have found that I have greatly injured my own piety by insisting too much on understanding everything before I would receive it; that is I have not been satisfied oftentimes with merely understanding that such things were asserted as facts, but was restless, unsatisfied, and unstable, unless I could comprehend and explain the philosophy of the facts. Surely this has formerly been my experience on the subject of the atonement. I found myself not satisfied with the bare announcement that Christ had died as my substitute, but I must understand the how and the why, and the great principles of divine government and the policy of Jehovah's empire on which this great transaction turned. I can indeed explain to my own satisfaction the philosophy of this transaction, and have often succeeded in explaining it to the most skeptical minds; but after all from subsequent reflection I have been persuaded that had the bare facts been pressed on them, and had they received it first as a fact on the authority of divine testimony, it would have been more healthful for their souls. Within the last year or two, I have been led more to consider the importance of holding forth facts as such until they are believed as facts, and then from time to time explaining their philosophy. I find this exceedingly healthful to my own soul, and to the souls of others, who first believe the facts without hearing the philosophy of them explained. This develops and strengthens faith. It leads them to feel that God is to be trusted, and that whatever he says is to be received barely on the authority of his own testimony. When afterwards the philosophy of it is opened to their view, they do not believe the fact any more firmly than before; but they are greatly edified, and even charmed with the philosophical illustrations of those things which before they have believed as facts on the authority of God. This I find to be exceedingly healthful to my own mind, and so far as I have had experience, to the minds of others. Indeed it is easy to see that the gospel should be presented and received in this way. This is the manner in which the Bible everywhere presents it. First, receive the facts as facts, simply because God affirms them; afterwards explain such as can be explained and comprehended, for the edification and growth in knowledge of God's dear children. But reverse the process: first, explain everything, and there is really no room left for faith; and if there is, you will find that professed converts really have no faith, and will either wholly reject or hold very loosely and doubtfully every declared fact or doctrine of the Bible which does not admit of clear philosophical analysis and explanation. This I am sure is the result of too much philosophizing and metaphysical speculation in preaching.

But let me say again that this kind of preaching is very pleasing to certain classes of hearers, although the truly and highly spiritual will soon find themselves growing lean on it. Yet a congregation generally will be puffed up, pleased, and from sermon to sermon think themselves greatly edified and benefitted; whereas it will generally be seen that they do not grow more prevalent in prayer, more humble, more consecrated to God; do not attain more of the meekness of a child and more of the patience of Jesus Christ. Their growth is not truly Christian growth. It is rather a philosophical growth, and oftentimes pride and egotism are the most prominent characteristics of a congregation who are fed with philosophy and metaphysics instead of the humbling facts of the gospel. I surely have been guilty enough in this respect, and I am certainly not alone in this condemnation, although others who have taken the same course substantially that I have in this respect, may not have seen their error so fully as I have been forced to see it. I wish not to be misunderstood. I would be far from advocating a mere presentation of facts without any explanation at all. I would take a middle course, so as on the one hand, not to puff up by a disproportionate development of the intelligence, while almost no room is left for the exercise of faith in divine testimony; nor on the other hand to stultify the intelligence by simply holding forth facts for the exercise of faith.

Your brother,

C. G. Finney

April 23, 1845

Dear Brethren:

Another error which has prevailed to a considerable extent in promoting revivals of religion, I apprehend, is that of encouraging an unhealthy degree of excitement. Some degree of excitement is inevitable. The truths that must be seen and duly appreciated to induce the sinner to turn to God, will of necessity produce a considerable degree of excitement in his mind; but it should always be understood that excitement, especially where it exists in a high degree, exposes the sinner to great delusions. Religion consists in the heart's obedience to the law of the intelligence, as distinguished from its being influenced by emotion or fear. When the feelings are greatly excited, the will yields to them almost of necessity. I do not mean that it does absolutely by necessity, but that an excited state of feeling has so much power over the will that it almost certainly controls it. Now the mind is never religious when it is actuated by the feelings, for this is following impulse. Whatever the feelings are, if the soul gives itself up to be controlled by feelings rather than by the law and gospel of God, as truth lies revealed in the intelligence, it is not a religious state of mind. Now the real difficulty of obeying the law of the intelligence is in proportion to the amount of excitement. Just in proportion as the feelings are strongly excited they tend to govern the will, and in as far as they do govern the will, there is and can be no religion in the soul, whatever these feelings are. Now just so much excitement is important in revivals as is requisite to secure the fixed and thorough attention of the mind to the truth, and no more. When excitement goes beyond this, it is always dangerous. When excitement is very great, so as really to carry the will, the subjects of this excitement invariably deceive themselves. They get the idea that they are religious in proportion as they are governed by their feelings. They are conscious of feeling deeply, and of acting accordingly, and because they do feel. They are conscious of being sincerely actuated by their feelings. This they regard as true religion. Whereas if they are really governed by their feelings as distinguished from their intelligence, they are not religious at all.

This is no doubt the secret of so many false hopes, in those revivals in which there is very great excitement. Where this has not been understood, and very great excitement has been rather nourished than controlled; where it has been taken for granted, that the revival of religion is great in proportion to the amount of excitement, great evils have invariably resulted to the cause of Christ. The great excitement attending revivals is an evil often incidental to real revivals of religion. But if the attention of the people can be thoroughly secured, no more excitement should be encouraged than is consistent with leaving the intelligence to exercise its full power on the will, without the obstruction of deeply excited feelings. I have often seen persons in so much excitement that the intelligence seemed to be almost stultified, and anything but reason seemed to have the control of the will. This is not religion, but enthusiasm; and oftentimes, as I shall have occasion to show in the course of these letters, has taken on at last the type of fanaticism.

Again, it is a dangerous thing in revivals to address too exclusively the hopes and fears of men, for the plain reason that selfish as man is, addressing his hopes and fears almost exclusively, tends to beget in him a selfish submission to God—a selfish religion to which he is moved on the one hand by fear of punishment, and on the other by hope of reward. Now it is true that God addresses the hopes and the fears of men, threatens them with punishment if they disobey, and offers them rewards if they obey, but still there is no virtue while the

heart is actuated merely by hope of reward or fear of
punishment. If sinners will disinterestedly love him and
consecrate themselves to the good of universal being, he
promises them a reward for this disinterested service.
But he nowhere promises them reward for following him
for the loaves and fishes. This is sheer selfishness. If sinners will repent and turn away from their sins, and disinterestedly consecrate themselves to the good of the universe and the glory of God, he promises to forgive their
sins. But this promise is not made to a selfish giving up
of sin. Outward sin may be given up from selfish
motives, but the sin of the heart never can be, for that
consists in selfishness, and it is nonsense and absurdity
to speak of really giving up sin from selfish motives.
Every selfish effort at giving up the heart is only a confir-
mation of selfishness. All attempts to give up sin from
mere fear of punishment or hope of reward are not only
hypocritical but tend directly to confirm, strengthen and
perpetuate the selfishness of the heart. There can be no
doubt that when sinners are careless, addressing their
hopes and fears is the readiest and perhaps the only way
of arousing them and getting their attention to the subject of salvation; but it should be forever remembered
that when their attention is thus secured, they should,
as far as possible, be kept from taking a selfish view of
the subject. Those considerations should then be pressed
on them that tend to draw them away from themselves
and constrain them to give their whole being up to God.
We should present to their minds the character of God,
his government, Christ, the Holy Spirit, the plan of salvation, any such thing that is calculated to charm the
sinner away from his sins, and from pursuing his own interests, and that is calculated to excite him to exercise
disinterested and universal love. On the other hand, his
own deformity, selfishness, self-will, pride, ambition,
enmity, lusts, guilt, loathsomeness, hatefulness, spiritual death; dependence, its nature and its extent; all

these things should be brought to bear in a burning focus on his mind. Right over against his own selfishness, enmity, self-will, and loathsome depravity, should be set the disinterestedness, the great love, the infinite compassion, the meekness, condescension, purity, holiness, truthfulness, and justice, of the blessed God. These should be held before him like a mirror until they press on him with such mountain weight as to break his heart. It is very easy to see that this cannot be done without producing a considerable degree and oftentimes a high degree of excitement. But it should be forever remembered that great excitement is only an incidental evil, and by no means a thing which is to be looked upon as highly favorable to his conversion. The more calm the soul can be kept while it gazes on those truths, the more free is the will left to comply with obligation as it lies revealed in the intelligence.

I have no doubt that much unreasonable opposition has been made to the excitement that is often witnessed in connection with revivals of religion, for, as I have said, great excitement is oftentimes unavoidable. But I have just as little doubt that oftentimes excitement has been unnecessarily great, and that real pains have been taken to promote deep and overwhelming excitements. I have sometimes witnessed efforts that were manifestly intended to create as much excitement as possible, and not unfrequently have measures been used which seemed to have no tendency to instruct or to subdue the will, or to bring sinners to the point of intelligently closing in with the terms of salvation; but on the contrary, it has seemed to me to beget a sort of infatuation through the power of overwhelming excitement. I cannot believe that this is healthful or at all safe in revivals. Indeed, where such a course has been taken, I believe it will be found to be a universal truth that evil instead of good has resulted from such efforts. The more I have seen of revivals, the more I am impressed with the importance of keeping excitement down as far as is consistent with a full, thorough and powerful exhibition of truth.

Oftentimes excitement spreads rapidly through a congregation under the influence of sympathy, and it not unfrequently becomes necessary in powerful revivals to proceed with great discretion for this reason. Where one individual becomes overwhelmed with excitement, and breaks out into loud crying and tears, where he cannot contain himself but has to wail out with excitement. It requires much judgment to dispose of such a case without injury on the one side or the other. If the thing be severely rebuked, it will almost invariably beget such a feeling among Christians as to quench the Spirit. On the other hand, if it be openly encouraged and the flame fanned, it will often produce an overwhelming amount of excitement throughout the congregation. Many will perhaps be entirely overcome, and multitudes will profess to submit to God; whereas scarcely one of them has acted intelligently or will in the end be found to have been truly converted. It is sometimes said that it doesn't matter how great the excitement is if it is produced by truth. Now it often comes to pass that up to a certain point, excitement will be produced by truth, at which point the intellect becomes bewildered, the sensibility becomes inflamed and overwhelmed, and there is a perfect explosion of feeling, while the intellect is almost smothered and wrecked by the tornado of excitement. Now this is a state very unfavorable to true conversion. I have seen such cases repeatedly, and before I had experience on that subject, I thought well and even highly of cases of this kind. But I have learned to view them in a different light and to feel much more confidence in apparent conversions that occur where there is greater calmness of mind. I wish to be understood. Excitement cannot reasonably be objected to as a thing entirely unnecessary in revivals; but the thing I would be distinctly understood to say is, that no effort should be made to produce excitement beyond what a lucid and powerful exposition of truth will produce. All the measures used to awaken interest, and our whole policy in regulating this awakened interest should be such as will not disturb the operations of the intelligence or divert its attention from the truth to which the heart is bound to submit.

I remark again that many excitements which are taken for revivals of religion, after all result in very little substantial piety, simply because the excitement is too great. Appeals are made too much to the feelings. Hope and fear are too exclusively addressed, a strain of preaching is adopted which appeals rather to the sympathies and the feelings than to the intelligence. A tornado of excitement results, but no intelligent action of the heart. The will is swept along by a tempest of feeling. The intelligence is rather for the time being stultified and confounded than possessed with clear views of truth. Now this certainly can never result in good.

Again, especially has this mistake been common, if I am not mistaken, in endeavors to promote revivals among children. The whole tendency of things with them is to excitement, and not the least dependence can be placed on revivals among them, without the greatest pains to instruct rather than to excite them. They may be thrown into a perfect tempest of excitement, and multitudes of them profess to be and perhaps appear to be converted, when they are influenced solely by their feelings, and have no thorough discriminating and correct views of truth at all. Now the result of all such efforts and such excitements among children is to make them skeptics, and indeed this is the result among all classes of persons who are brought to be the subjects of great excitement about religion and have not sufficient solid and discriminating instruction to turn their hearts to God. Such evils are doubtless to be looked upon among the greatest evils with which communities are ever visited.

Your brother,

C. G. Finney

Chapter II

REVIVAL ENTHUSIASM

Dear Brethren:

I am by no means done with the subject of *excitement* as connected with revivals of religion. In every age of the church, cases have occurred in which persons have had such clear manifestations of divine truth as to prostrate their physical strength entirely. This appears to have been the case with Daniel. He fainted and was unable to stand. Saul of Tarsus seems to have been overwhelmed and prostrated under the blaze of divine glory that surrounded him. I have met with many cases where the physical powers were entirely prostrated by a clear apprehension of the infinitely great and weighty truths of religion.

With respect to these cases I remark:

1. That they are not cases of that objectionable excitement of which I spoke in my last letter. For in these cases, the intelligence does not appear to be stultified and confused, but to be full of light. The mind seems not to be conscious of any unusual excitement of its own sensibility; but on the contrary, seems to itself to be calm and its state seems peculiar only because truth is seen with unusual clearness. Manifestly there is no such effervescence of the sensibility as produces tears, or any of the usual manifestations of an excited imagination or deeply moved feelings. There is not that gush of feeling which distracts the thoughts, but the mind sees truth unveiled, and in such relations as really to take away all bodily strength, while the mind looks in upon the unveiled glories of the Godhead. The veil seems to be removed from the mind, and truth is seen much as we must suppose it to be when the spirit is disembodied. No wonder this should overpower the body.

Now such cases have often stumbled those who have witnessed them; and yet so far as I have had opportunity to enquire into their subsequent history, I have been persuaded that in general these were sound cases of conversion. A few may possibly be counterfeits; but I do not recollect any clearly marked case of this kind in which it was not afterwards manifest that the love of God had been deeply shed abroad in the heart, the will greatly subdued, and the whole character greatly and most desirably modified.

Now I again remark that I do not feel at liberty to object to these cases of excitement, if they may be so called. Whatever excitement attends them seems to result necessarily from the clear manifestations which God makes to the soul. This excitement, instead of being boisterous, unintelligent and enthusiastic, like that alluded to in my former letter, seems to be similar to that which we may suppose exists among the departed spirits of the just. Indeed this seems to me a just principle: *we need fear no kind or degree of excitement which is produced simply by perceived truth, and is consistent with the healthful operation of the intellectual powers.* Whatever exceeds this must be disastrous.

In general, those cases of bodily prostration of which I have spoken occur without the apparent intervention of any external means adapted to produce such a result. So far as I have observed, they occur when the soul is shut up to God. In the case of Daniel, of Saul, of Wm. Tennant, and others there were no human instrumentalities, or measures, or exciting appeals to the imagination or sensibility, but a simple revelation of God to the soul by the Holy Ghost.

Now the excitement produced in this manner seems to be of a very different kind from that produced by very boisterous, vociferous preaching, exhortation, or prayer: or by those very exciting appeals to fear which are often made by zealous exhorters or preachers. Exciting measures are often used and very exciting illustrations are employed, which agitate and strain the nervous system until the sensibility seems to gush forth like a flood of water, and for the time completely overwhelm and drown the intelligence.

But the excitement produced when the Holy Ghost reveals God to the soul is totally different from this. It is not only consistent with the clearest and most enlarged perceptions of the intelligence, but directly promotes and produces such perceptions. Indeed it promotes the free and unembarrassed action of both the intelligence and the will.

This is the kind of excitement that we need. It is that which the Holy Spirit always produces. It is not an excitement of sympathy; not a spasm, or explosion of the nervous sensibility, but is a calm, deep, sacred flow of the soul in view of the clear, infinitely important and impressive truths of God.

It requires often no little discrimination to distinguish between an effervescence of the sensibility produced by loud and exciting appeals; by corresponding measures on the one hand, and on the other that calm, but deep and sometimes overpowering flow of soul which is produced by the Spirit of God revealing Jesus to the soul. I have sometimes feared that these different kinds of excitement are confounded with each other, and consequently by one class of persons all alike, rejected and denounced, and by another class wholly defended. Now it appears to me of great importance to distinguish in these cases between things that differ.

When I see cases of extraordinary excitement I have learned to enquire as calmly and affectionately as I can into the views of truth taken by the mind at the time. If the individual readily and spontaneously gives such reasons as naturally account for this excitement, I can then judge of its character. If it really originates in clear views presented by the Holy Ghost, of the character of God and of the great truths of his government, the mind will be full of these truths and will spontaneously give them off whenever there is ability to utter them. It will be seen that there is a remarkably clear view of truth, and where power of speech is left, a remarkable facility in communicating it. As a general thing I do not fear the excitement in these cases however great it may be.

But where the attention seems to be occupied with one's own feelings, and when they can give no intelligible reason for feeling as they do, very little confidence can be placed in their state. I have frequently seen cases when the excitement was very great, and almost overwhelming; yet the subject of it upon the closest enquiry could give no intelligent account of any perceptions of truth which the mind had. The soul seemed to be moved to its deepest foundations; but not by clear exhibitions of truth or by manifestations of God to the soul. Hence the mind did not seem to be acting intelligently. I have learned to be afraid of this and to place little or no confidence in professed conversions under such circumstances. I have observed that the subjects of these excitements will after a season look upon themselves as having been infatuated and swept away by a tornado of unintelligent excitement.

ILLUSTRATION: A FACT

As an illustration of what I would say upon this subject I will relate a fact that once occurred under my own observation. I attended a camp-meeting in the State of New York which had been in progress two or three days before my arrival. I heard the preachers and attended the exercises through most of that day, and there appeared to be very little—indeed no visible excitement. After several sermons had been preached and after much exhortation, prayer and singing, I observed several of the leading men to be whispering to each other for some time as if in profound deliberation, after which one of them, a man of athletic frame and stentorian voice came down from the stand and pressed his way along into the midst of a company of women who were sitting in front of the stand, and then began to clap his hands and halloo at the top of his voice: power! power!! power!!! Soon, another and another set in, till there was a general shouting and clapping of hands, followed presently by the shrieking of women, and resulting after a little time in the falling of several of them from their seats. Then it was proclaimed that the power of God was revealed from heaven. After pushing this excitement to a most extraordinary extent, the minister who began it and those who united with him and had thus succeeded as they supposed in bringing down the power of God upon the congregation, retired from the scene of confusion manifestly much gratified at the result.

This scene and some others of a similar character have often occurred to my mind. I cannot but regard such movements as calculated to promote anything else than true religion. In the getting up of this excitement there was not a word of truth communicated; there was no prayer or exhortation—nothing but a most vociferous shouting of power! power!! power!!! accompanied by an almost deafening clapping of hands. I believe this to have been an extraordinary case and that probably but few cases occur which are so highly objectionable. But things often occur in revivals which seem to beget an excitement but little more intelligent than this. Such appeals are made to the imagination and to certain departments of the sensibility as completely to throw the action of the intellect into the shade. So far as such efforts to promote revivals are made, they are undoubtedly highly disastrous, and should be entirely discouraged.

Your brother,

C. G. Finney

May 21, 1845

Dear Brethren:

While upon the subject of excitement I wish to make a few suggestions on the danger that highly excited feelings will take a wrong direction and result in fanaticism. Everyone is aware that when the feelings are strongly excited, they are capable of being turned in various directions and of assuming various types according to the circumstances of the excited individual. Few persons who have witnessed revivals of religion have not had occasion to remark this tendency of the human mind, and the efforts of Satan to use it for his own advantage, by mingling in the spirit of fanaticism with the spirit of a religious revival.

Fanaticism results from what a certain writer calls "loveless light." Whenever the mind is enlightened in regard to what men ought to be and do and say, and is not at the same time in the exercise of benevolence, a spirit of fanaticism, indignation, rebuke, and denunciation is the almost inevitable result.

By fanaticism I mean a state of mind in which the malign emotions take the control of the will, and hurry the individual away into an outrageous and vindictive effort to sustain what he calls right and truth. He contends for what he regards as truth or right with a malign spirit.

Now in seasons of religous revival there is special danger that fanaticism will spring up under the influence of infernal agency. It is in many respects a peculiarly favorable time for Satan to sow in a rank soil the seed of some of the most turbulent and outrageous forms of error that have ever cursed the world.

Among the crowd who attend preaching at such times, there are almost always persons who have a strong fanatical tendency of mind. They are strongly inclined to censoriousness, faultfinding, vituperation, denunciation and rebuke. It is a strong and ultra democratic tendency of mind, anti-conservative in the extreme and strongly tending to misrule. Now in proportion as persons of this character become enlightened respecting the duties and the sins of men, they are very likely to break forth into a spirit of turbulent fanaticism.

It is well known that almost all the reforms of this and of every age have been cursed by this sort of fanaticism. Temperance, Moral Reform, Physiological and Dietetic Reform, Anti-Slavery—all have felt the blight; almost nothing has escaped. When lecturers or others take up these questions and discuss them, pouring light upon the public mind, it often seems to disturb a cockatrice's den. The deep and perhaps hitherto hidden tendencies to fanaticism are blown up into flame, and often burst forth as from the molten heart of a volcano. Their indignation is aroused: their censorious and vituperative tongues are let loose; those unruly members that set on fire the course of nature and are set on fire of hell, seem to pour forth a stream of burning lava to scorch and desolate society. Their prayers, their exhortations, everything they say or do, are but a stream of scolding, fault-finding, and recrimination. They insist upon it, they do well to be angry—that to manifest anything less than the utmost indignation were profane, and suited neither to the subject nor the occasion.

Now it is remarkable to what an extent this class of minds have been brought forward by the different reforms of the day and even by revivals of religion. No matter what the subject is—if it be the promotion of peace, they will contend for peace with the spirit of outrageous war. With their tongues they will make war upon everything that opposes them; pour forth unmeasured abuse upon all who disagree with them, and make no compromise nor hold any communion with those who cannot at once subscribe to their peculiar views. If the subject be Anti-slavery, they contend for it with the spirit of slaveholders; and while they insist that all men are free, they will allow freedom of opinion to none but themselves. They would enslave the views and sentiments of all who differ from them, and soon castigate them into an acquiescence with their own opinions.

In revivals of religion this spirit generally manifests itself in a kind of scolding and denunciatory way of praying for all classes of people. Next, in exhortation, preaching, or in conversation. It especially attacks ministers and the leading influences of the church, and moves right on progressively until it finally regards the visible church as Babylon, and all men as on the high road to hell who do not come out and denounce her.

Now this spirit often springs up in revivals so stealthily and insidiously that its true character is not at first detected. Perhaps the church *is* cold, the minister and leading influences are out of the way, and it seems no more than just, nay even necessary that some severity should be used towards those who are so far out of the way. The individual himself feels this so strongly that he does not suspect himself of fanaticism though he deals out a large measure of rebuke in which a sprinkling of the malign element is unconsciously mingled. He pleads the example of Christ, of apostles and prophets, and can quote many passages from the Bible very similar to those which he now uses, and deems himself justified in using inasmuch as they are drawn from scripture. He assumes their application as he applies them, and also that himself stands in God's stead and is the mouth of God in rebuking iniquity.

Now when this spirit first appears it grates across the tender minds of those who are in a spirit of love. At first it distresses and agonizes them, but by and by there seems to be so much truth in what is said; their prayers

and exhortations are so exciting; their own attention being directed to the faults that are so sternly rebuked,
they begin to drink in the same spirit and partake of that
boisterous and fiery zeal which was at first so inconsistent with the sweetness of their spirit. They begin to see
as they suppose, how the denunciations of the prophets
of Christ and of his apostles apply to those among whom
they live. Their attention is wholly engrossed with the
faults of the church and the ministry, and they can see
nothing good. They begin to doubt and query whether
the visible church are not all hypocrites. At first they
fear but soon believe that nearly all the ministers are self-
deceived, hirelings, conservatives, ambitious, stewards
of the devil. Church organizations are looked upon first
with suspicion, then with contempt and abhorrence.
"Coming out of Babylon" becomes the order of the day.

Fanaticism takes on a very great variety of types. Its
modifications are almost innumerable. From the spirit
of the crusades when men went forth with boots and
spurs, with fire and sword to convert their fellow men to
Christianity, down to the obscure professor of religion
who mutters in a corner his scolding and faultfinding
with everybody and everything, all the intervening space
is filled with the multiform phases of fanaticism. From
the fiery zeal with which the itinerant declaims, voci-
ferates and denounces both church and state, down to
the individual who rather looks than speaks out his
fanaticism, you may find this class of persons kindling
up and nursing the fires of fanaticism in almost every
corner of Christendom.

Now this is doubtless the spirit of Satan which he has
manifested in the church and in the world through all
past ages.

We have one able book on the subject of fanaticism;
but we need another which shall take up and expose its
more modern developments—which shall delineate as
on a page of light the workings of this dark spirit whose

malign influence, silently working like leaven, would fain leaven the whole lump and make this earth malign like hell. More of this at another time.

Your brother,

C. G. Finney

June 4, 1845

Dear Brethren:

I beg leave to call the attention of the brethren to the danger of revival preachers themselves introducing the spirit of fanaticism. When they meet with great opposition from the church or the world or the ministry, they sometimes indulge in a strain of remark that is strongly tinctured with bitterness, or at least, with the appearance of bitterness and denunciation. There are sometimes streaks and dashes of this in the preaching and spirit of good men. Satan seems to take advantage of their circumstances to infuse, imperceptibly to themselves, into their spirit and strain of preaching, praying and talking, a dash of bitterness and vituperation. This strongly tends to beget a fanatical state of mind in their admirers.

Revival preachers have sometimes been greatly opposed by ministers until they have become sore and somewhat irritable; and in this state of mind have sometimes gone so far as to preach and speak of those ministers in a very censorious spirit. This inevitably does great mischief in the revivals in which they are engaged. It catches like fire among the converts and among those professors who are most immediately under his influence, and tends strongly to run the revival out of the spirit of love, into a spirit of recrimination and bitterness. A sore and bitter state of mind will be manifested by those who think themselves engaged in the work of the Lord, while the spirit of meekness, gentleness, brotherly kindness and of deep and compassionate sympathy with Christ and with his church, will be almost entirely supplanted.

If I am not mistaken, revival preachers have often greatly erred in this matter. Whitfield sometimes did so, as he himself confesses, and the result was such as I have named, as everyone knows who has read the history of the revivals that occurred under his labors. There is not one among the revival preachers of modern times who has not erred to a greater or less extent in this respect. I am sure that I have sometimes done so; and I do not know of a revival preacher of whom I do not think that to some extent the remarks just made are applicable.

A little spice of this spirit in a revival preacher will work like leaven until it leavens the whole lump, and if indulged in, will sooner or later totally change the character of the excitement in which he labors until it will become a revival of arrant fanaticism instead of pure religion. This result may occur without his once suspecting that such is the tendency of his spirit, preaching and movements. Hence ere he is aware, the evil is too far developed to admit of a remedy.

It does appear to me that revival preachers should be exceedingly honest with themselves on this subject, and withal very guarded, forbearing, mild and conciliatory in their manner of speaking and preaching, especially concerning those who oppose their views and measures. It is often better to take no public notice whatever of opposition, and especially not to allude to opposers, and by no means to speak of or pray for ministers or Christians in such a way as may blow up into a flame the latent sparks of fanaticism that are smothered in so many bosoms.

In thinking of this subject, in looking over the state of the church, in reading the history of revivals of religion in all ages, I have been struck and deeply affected with the innumerable instances in which promoters of revivals have erred in substantially the manner I have described. They have unwittingly imbibed more or less of a spirit of fanaticism themselves, and it manifests itself so much in their public efforts as greatly to mar the work of the Lord and of course to grieve the Spirit of God. Indeed some revival preachers appear to me to have forsaken the right way without being aware of it, and really to have become highly fanatical in their spirit, preaching and general bearing, until God has manifestly been obliged to rebuke them by withdrawing his Spirit and closing the doors of the church against them. If revivals of pure religion are to be preserved from fanaticism, the utmost pains should be taken to preserve the leaders from this spirit. It is one of the grand devices of the devil to infuse this spirit stealthily into the leaders and thereby poison the revival to death.

In what I have said I would not be understood to intimate by any means that revival preachers alone have fallen into this error, for I am very confident that they have not so frequently fallen into it as some who have never promoted revivals of religion. The latter have more often fallen, for the reason that their general strain of preaching has so much of jangling, of controversy, of rebuke, censoriousness and bitterness against all who differ from them, that the Spirit of God seldom if ever refreshes the heritage to which they minister. I have known several such ministers who were far enough from being revival preachers, and whose preaching tended only to revive and perpetuate the spirit of fanaticism and rebuke. But what I have intended in this letter is, that revival preachers themselves have sometimes fallen into this error which is so common with many other preachers.

Indeed sectarianism in all its forms is only a modified species of fanaticism, as might easily be shown; and revival preachers who have connected sectarian movements with their revival operations have perhaps uniformly shown that a fanatical spirit was the result.

My brethren, let us be careful that our own spirit is heavenly, Christ-like—that we have the wisdom that cometh down from above, which is "first pure, then peaceable, gentle, full of mercy and good fruits." Let us labor in this spirit, and the result will show that we are workmen who need not be ashamed.

Your brother,

C. G. Finney

June 18, 1845

Dear Brethren:

If I am not entirely mistaken, many excitements that have been supposed to be revivals of religion, have after all had but very little true religion in them. It seems to have been nearly or quite overlooked, that all religion is love. And it is remarkable to see to what an extent, in some instances at least, there is a manifestation of fiery zeal, often tinctured strongly with bitterness and sarcasm, instead of the gentleness and sweetness that characterizes the true religion of Jesus. If you attend the meetings of any kind, if you converse with the brethren, with the professed converts, with any who are influenced by the excitement, you find that there is a strain of evil speaking, faultfinding and scolding which is anything but the true religion of Christ. There is to be sure a great excitement, a great deal of bustle and conversation, a great many means and measures, in short a great deal of everything calculated to promote a certain kind of excitement. There is indeed a powerful revival, but certainly not a revival of pure religion. Sinners are speaking in great bitterness of Christians, and professed Christians are speaking with very little less bitterness of them. The preaching is very much in a strain of vituperation, and this begets almost of course the like spirit and strain in everything else connected with the excitement. There seems to be in it a deep, turbid and bitter current of feeling, that is the very essence of fanaticism. The spirit of Satan, instead of the spirit of God, has, no doubt, been poured out on the people. It has been an outpouring of *a* spirit, but not of the Holy Spirit of God. It seems to be a going forth of infernal agencies, a letting loose of the powers of darkness, a season of deep delusions: and what is surprising is, that even good people are often for a time carried away with it, and for weeks and perhaps for months do not discover their mistake. As a brother who had himself been laboring under this mistake, expressed it—"I have been trying," said he, "to cast out devils through Beelzebub the prince of the devils."

You will very often see the evidence of this state of mind in the very countenances of those who are deeply excited. They look cross; there is a deep dissatisfaction of mind manifested in their countenances. You go to a prayer meeting, or other meeting where numbers who have this kind of excitement are assembled, and you will see a dark cloud gathering on the faces of the excited ones. Instead of that open, sweet, calm, meek, but deeply solemn and humble state of mind which invariably shows itself in the countenance, there is in the eye, and in all the features of the mind, a distracted, fanatical, determined look; a self-will and denunciatory expression that seems to say, "Stand by thyself, for I am holier than thou."

I hardly know how to describe what I have sometimes witnessed in such cases. And perhaps I cannot so describe it, as to make myself understood to any except those, who in the providence of God, have fallen under circumstances to witness it. Sometimes this state of mind will not be generally manifested, in an excitement. Perhaps a revival of pure religion commences, and there is no manifestation of this spirit at all. But I scarcely ever saw a powerful revival anywhere without seeing more or less of a fanatical spirit in the course of the revival, manifesting itself in one or more cases.

If the leader in such revivals keeps himself entirely clear of this spirit, and watches its development narrowly on every side round about, and is entirely faithful and timely in private and personal expostulation and warning, in the case of those who are seized with it, it can no doubt generally be prevented.

It will not unfrequently manifest itself at first in prayer meetings, if liberty is given; or if liberty is not given for anyone to pray who feels disposed, you will sometimes see a man or woman break forth in a prodigiously excited manner, and let off in a torrent of vituperation in their prayers. There will be in it a strain of bitterness that will be very shocking to all who do not deeply sympathize with such a state of mind. Now if the minister at once goes to that man or woman immediately after meeting, has a plain and affectionate conversation, and sets before the individual the true state of his mind, he may succeed in the outset in so opening his eyes, as to detect the delusion and save him from further evil. But if he neglect it, the evil will spread rapidly, the delusions will increase in the mind of the individual himself, and probably in the course of a few days, or at the utmost, weeks, it will completely change the type of the revival, grieve away the Spirit of God, and let in a flood of infernal agencies to desolate the church.

I hope my brethren will not understand from what I have said and intend to say on the subject of fanaticism, as it often appears in connection with revivals, anything that shall give occasion to speak reproachfully of the most faithful and pungent dealing with the consciences of backsliders and impenitent sinners.

I am aware, and who that has ever seen revivals is not aware, that the spirit of complaining, faultfinding, and censoriousness, is by no means confined to those who are endeavoring to promote the excitement or revival, and that the spirit of fanaticism is by no means confined to this class of persons. It is often more appallingly manifested among those who partake not at all of the spirit of promoting revivals. It is very common indeed to see the opposers of revivals both in and out of the church, manifesting at such times, a most turbulent and intolerant spirit, and a form of fanaticism, not less disgraceful and unreasonable than that to which I have alluded.

Sometimes even ministers, prominent professors of religion, as well as those without the church and who are opposed to the revival or excitement, or whatever its character may be, are seen to be filled with the spirit of caviling, censoriousness, complaining and faultfinding, and whose minds seem occupied almost altogether with real or apparent, or at least, imagined defects in the spirit of those who are engaged in promoting the work, or in the means used by them.

It is very common to hear this class of persons find fault with really the most unobjectionable things—they seem to have the spirit of calling evil good, and good evil. Anything like faithful and pungent dealing, anything like a thorough searching and probing the heart of backsliders and sinners, to the bottom, is by them called abusive, personal, vituperative, and such like things.

Now what I desire to say, brethren, is this, that there are great dangers, and oftentimes great errors on both sides to be apprehended and guarded against. I have already intimated that the spirit of fanaticism, as it appears in those who are endeavoring to promote a revival, is generally provoked and developed by a spirit of fanaticism, opposed to the revival. An unreasonable opposition on the part of others, seems to develop oftentimes, in those who are trying to promote the work a spirit really hostile the work itself.

For my own part I have seldom seen a spirit of fanaticism manifest itself among promoters of revivals, only as it was provoked and developed by a spirit of opposition to revivals. When opposition takes on certain forms, and if found to exist among ministers and leading professors of religion, there is then the greatest danger that the good and the praying people will be overcome of evil, instead of overcoming evil with good. This should be always guarded against.

Your brother,

C. G. Finney

July 2, 1845

Dear Brethren:

I have yet many things to say on the subject of the appearance of a fanatical spirit, in connection with revivals. The particular thing to which I would now call the attention of the brethren, is this. There is a class of minds, that in seasons of deep excitement, and especially when there is a good deal of preaching on the necessity and reality of divine influences, the spirit of prayer, being led by the Spirit, being filled with the Spirit, etc., who are extremely apt to give themselves up to be led by impulses. Mistaking the true manner in which the Spirit of God influences the mind, and not realizing that he enlightens the intelligence, and leads the Christian who is under his influence to be eminently reasonable, and rational in all his views and movements, they are looking for the Spirit to make direct impressions on their feelings, and to lead them through the influence of their feelings and not through the intelligence. Hence they are very full of impressions. One has an impression that he ought to do such a thing, or say such a thing, to go to such a place, to visit a tavern for instance, and converse with the inmates of a bar room, or to go and rebuke a minister, or to tell the elders or deacons of the church, that God has revealed it to him that they are right in the way of the revival—in short, there is no end to the forms in which these delusions appear. Sometimes they are impressed with the conviction that they ought to get up and interrupt the speaker, during public preaching, or that they ought to break forth in prayer under circumstances that would manifestly introduce disorder—and many such like things are very liable to occur in seasons of deep excitement in revivals of religion. Sometimes they will have particular views presented to their imaginations—that such a minister is right in the way, and leading all the souls under his influence down to hell—that terrible judgments are coming on the place—that the revival is about to cease—or that some other terrible thing is about to take place. Now if this spirit is watched, it is remarkable to see how uniformly it will take on a severe, denunciatory and turbulent type. It is remarkable to see how often it will manifest its principal hostility and opposition towards the leading and most efficient influences that are at work in promoting a genuine revival of religion. If this spirit be narrowly watched, it will soon be seen, that it is really opposition to all that is truly good in the work; and that oftentimes its opposition to the highest and best influences employed by the Spirit in the promotion of the revival, is truly shocking. Probably few persons who have seen powerful revivals of religion, have not witnessed with pain and astonishment, things similar to those I have described.

Now these things are exceedingly dangerous in a revival, for the reason that they often appear among those who have been regarded as most engaged in the work, most spiritual and prayerful. They often occur in connection with experiences, or rather succeed experiences, that were manifestly truly Christian and highly spiritual.

Now with respect to these things let me remark:

1. That oftentimes when persons are really in a spiritual frame of mind, when they are really simple-hearted, unsuspicious, and willing to be led in any direction, Satan often succeeds, by transforming himself into an angel of light, in persuading them to give themselves up to impulses and impressions; and from that moment, he leads them captive at his will.

2. I remark that as a general rule, the influence of Satan in these things may be distinguished from the influences of the Holy Spirit by this—a mere impression that you must do this or that thing, go and converse with this person or that person, go to this place or that place, is by no means to be regarded. When the Spirit of God leads an individual to take a peculiar interest, feel peculiar compassion and drawing of heart in prayer and labor for particular individuals, this influence may be safely trusted. If you find yourself drawn out in mighty

prayer for certain individuals, exercised with great compassion, agonized with strong crying and tears, for a certain family or neighborhood or people, let such an influence be yielded to. If it is all compassion, an affectionate zeal for their salvation, a deep and affectionate interest in their spiritual welfare, you may safely take it for granted that this is from God, and give the mind and the outward developments up to its influence, and put forth all the efforts that may appear reasonable to secure their salvation. But let mere impressions unconnected with love, compassion, with the spirit of prayer, etc., be strongly guarded against, for to say the least, as a general rule, such impressions are not from God. It would not, perhaps, be too much to say that they never are. God's Spirit leads men by the intelligence, and not through mere impressions made on the sensibility. When the guilt and the danger of an individual is strongly set before the mind, when the great value of his soul is made to be clearly apprehended, when the heart is drawn out in prayer for his conversion and salvation, this is indeed from God. I have known some cases where persons have rendered themselves highly ridiculous, have greatly injured their own souls, and the cause of God, by giving themselves up to an enthusiastic and fanatical following of impressions.

Your brother,

C. G. Finney

Chapter III

INFREQUENCY OF REVIVALS

Dear Brethren:

I am rejoiced to perceive that the inquiry is beginning to agitate the Church: Why are there not more revivals? as well as: Why is their character so changed? The inquiry is also made: What can be done to promote them? and to promote them under a desirable and permanent type.

Now, my dear brethren, I hope and trust that you will not be offended with me, if I speak my mind on this subject with great plainness. The circumstances of the Church, the decline of revivals, and the whole aspect of the Christian world, demand it.

I have seen in the public papers various reasons assigned for this declension of revivals, this absence of revival influence, this powerless preaching of the gospel.

Now it does appear to me that we who are ministers, instead of looking abroad and searching for the fundamental difficulty beyond and out of ourselves, should see that whatever else may be an occasion of the great falling off and decline in revivals, our own spiritual state is certainly one, if not the primary and fundamental reason of this decline. Want of personal holiness, unction, power in prayer, and in preaching the word—the want of holy living and consecration to the work—of self-denial, and energetic effort in the ministry—these, no doubt, are the principal reasons why revivals are so few and far between, and of so superficial character at the present day.

The fact is, ministers have turned aside, in a great degree, to vain jangling; have given up their attention to church-politics, church-government, and ecclesiastical proceedings of various kinds. The ministers have been diverted to an alarming and most injurious extent, from promoting revivals of religion out of the Church, and holiness in the Church.

I appeal to you, my brethren, of all denominations, if it is not a fact in your own experience and observation, that ministers have to a great and alarming extent suffered themselves to be diverted from the direct work of promoting the conversion of sinners and sanctification of the Church. This is too notorious to need any proof. The Journals of the day, the movements of ecclesiastical bodies, the doctrinal collisions, and, shall I say?, ambitious projects, that have come up and figured before the public, within the last few years, bear no dubious testimony to the fact that the great mass of ministers are turned aside from promoting revivals, and the holiness and entire consecration of the Church.

Now, my beloved brethren, while this is so, does it not become us to take this home, confess it, bewail it, and first of all understand that whatever else needs to be corrected and set right, we must ourselves repent and receive a new unction for the work.

Beloved brethren, it is of no use for us to go abroad and search for reasons, while the principal of all the reasons lies at our own door. While our hearts are cold, our zeal in revivals abated, while we are turned aside, and running here and there to attend conventions, councils, ecclesiastical bodies; while we are engaged in reading the vituperative publications of the day, and entering into church-politics and janglings about church-government and all these things, it is no wonder that both the Church and the world are asleep on the subject of revivals.

Until the leaders enter into the work, until the ministry are baptized with the Holy Spirit, until we are awake and in the field with our armour on, and our souls anointed with the Holy Spirit, it certainly ill becomes us to be looking around at a distance for the cause of the decline of revivals.

I have no doubt that there are many causes, which, the Lord willing, we will search out. But this is the first, the greatest, the most God-dishonoring of all—that the ministry are not in the work, that the shepherds have in a measure forsaken their flocks, that is, they are not leading them into the green pastures and beside the still waters—are not themselves so anointed and full of faith and power, as to be instrumental in leading the Church into the field for the promotion of revivals.

To a considerable extent the churches seem not to be well aware of the state of the ministry, and for the reasons that they themselves are in a state of decline. The decline of vital godliness in the ministry has been of course the occasion of so much decline in the churches that they are hardly aware either of their own state or of the spiritual state of the ministry.

Now, my dear brethren, I hope it will not be said, that by writing in this way, I am letting down the influence of the ministry and encouraging a faultfinding spirit in the Church. I would by no means do this. But I think that we may rest assured that unless we are frank enough, and humble enough, and honest enough, to look the true state of things in the face, confess, forsake our sins, and return to the work and engage in the promotion of revivals, God will undoubtedly rebuke us, will raise up other instruments to do his work, and set us aside; will alienate the heart of the churches from us, destroy our influence with them, and raise up we know not whom, to go forth and possess the land.

Among all the conventions of the present day, I have thought that one of a different character from any that have been, might be greatly useful. If we could have a ministerial convention for prayer, confessing our faults one to another, and getting into a revival spirit, and devising the best ways and means for the universal promotion of revivals throughout the length and breadth of the land, I should rejoice in it. It has appeared to me that of all the conventions of the day, one of this kind might be the most useful.

What shall we say, brethren? Are we not greatly in fault? Have not the ministry, to a great extent, lost the spirit of revivals? Is there not a great lack of unction and power amongst us? And have we not suffered ourselves to be greatly and criminally diverted from this great work?

If so, my dear brethren, shall we not return? shall we not see our fault, confess it to the churches, to the world, and return; and in the name of the Lord lift up our banner?

Your brother,

C. G. Finney

August 14, 1845

Dear Brethren:

I hope my brethren will bear with me, while I further insist on the general delinquency of ministers, especially of late, in regard to revivals.

There has been so manifest and so lamentable a falling off from a revival spirit among the ministers of Christ as to become a matter of general, if not universal observation. Nothing is more common than the remark, that ministers, as a general fact, have lost the spirit of revivals, have become very zealous in ecclesiastical matters, censorious, afraid of revivals, of revival men and measures, and that they do little or nothing directly for the promotion of revivals of religion. Now I do not think that this is a universal fact, but as a general remark it is too obvious to need proof, and I think must be conceded by all.

Now, dearly beloved brethren, unless there is a spirit of revival in the ministry, it is in vain to expect it in the church. The proper place for the shepherd, is before or in advance of the sheep. The sheep will follow him whithersoever he goes, but if he attempt to drive them before him, he will scatter them in every direction. If the shepherd fall away from a revival spirit, the sheep will naturally decline also. If he advance in the work of the Lord, they will almost as a thing of course follow him.

The greatest of all difficulties in the way of the promotion of revivals has been, a superficial work of grace in the hearts of ministers themselves. If this is not true I am greatly mistaken.

My brethren, believe me, I speak not this censoriously, or in the spirit of faultfinding; it is the full and deliberate conviction of my own mind—an opinion formed not hastily, but from protracted observation, and from an intimate acquaintance with great numbers of the ministers of Christ of different denominations.

While the ministers of Christ are filled with the Spirit of God, the Church, as a general thing, will not backslide. I say as a general thing; there may in some instances be influences brought to bear on the churches, that will divert them from the promotion of holiness in their own hearts and the conversion of the impenitent, in spite of all that the most wakeful and vigilant ministry can do. Great political excitements, great commercial embarrassments, great depressions or elevations in the business and pecuniary state of the Church or the world, may, in a great measure, divert the mass of professors of religion for a time from deep spirituality, although the ministers may be awake. And yet it is my deliberate opinion that a thoroughly wakeful, prayerful, energetic ministry by their influence would generally if not universally prevent all the calamities and disturbances by so deeply engaging the Church and the community in general on religious subjects, that war, great political excitements, great commercial excitements, speculations or embarrassments would not be likely to occur. However this may be, I cannot believe it to be otherwise than a general truth, that if the ministry are baptized with the Holy Spirit, and deeply anointed with the revival influence, so the Church will be—"like priest, like people."

And now brethren, it does seem to me that when we ourselves are thoroughly in a revival spirit, our call to the churches to arise and engage in the general promotion of revivals, will be immediately responded to on the part of the Church. Let the ministry only come out in the true spirit of revivals, and I doubt whether any minister in the land can preach for three sabbaths to his church in the Spirit, without finding the spirit of revival waking up in the Church. Let this experiment once be tried; let us wake up to the importance of this subject, confess and forsake our own sins, and cry aloud to the Church, and spare not; let us lift up our voice like a trumpet, and rally the hosts of God's elect; and if they are deaf to the call, then let us inquire most earnestly what is next to be done. But until we are anointed to the work, do not let us tempt the Lord or abuse the Church, by looking out of ourselves, and away from ourselves for the cause of decline in revivals.

Do not misunderstand me. I know that the Church is in a state of decline, and needs greatly to be quickened and aroused; but I am confident that the prime cause of this decline in the Church is to be found in the fact that the ministers have been diverted from their appropriate work. And I am also confident that the only remedy for this state of things is first and foremost of all, for ministers to come into a deeply spiritual and revived state of mind. And as soon as this comes to pass, there will be a general revival. And I am not looking for it to come unless ministers do thoroughly wake up to their own state, and the state of the Church.

Your brother,

C. G. Finney

Chapter IV

THE CAUSE OF DECLINE IN REVIVALS

Dear Brethren:

Another cause of the decline of revivals, in my estimation, is that a right course has not been pursued with the churches. In some instances they have been urged to labor and visit, and put forth active efforts for the conversion of sinners, while they have had very little wholesome food to live upon. Much labor has been demanded with too spare a diet. They have heard very little else than mere legal preaching. Ministers have been preaching almost exclusively to the impenitent, and perhaps for months have given the church scarcely one wholesome meal of the real gospel. If Christians are to labor for God and souls they must be fed with a plenty of the bread that cometh down from heaven—they must be made to know and feel where their great strength lies—must have Christ in all his offices, and relations, and fullness, frequently presented to them. If this course is not pursued, their own piety will not only greatly suffer, but they will come into a legal spirit and all their efforts for the conversion of sinners will be only bustle and legality; and in this state they may encompass sea and land to make proselytes, and fill the church with spurious converts.

If I am not entirely mistaken, this has been, to an alarming extent, the fact in revivals that have prevailed within the last few years. Christians have had so little of the Gospel that they have become legal, self-righteous, blustering, carnal, mechanical, unbelieving; and their efforts have made converts like themselves; which has brought revivals into great disrepute.

Again, ministers by preaching too exclusively to the impenitent, and dwelling so little on the marrow and fatness and fulness of the gospel, have greatly suffered in their own piety—have themselves become, in many instances, legal, hard-hearted, and censorious. In this state they cannot promote true revivals of religion. Not living themselves on Christ, not dwelling in God and God in them they are in no state to feed the church or promote true and thorough revivals of religion.

Again, there has been so great a fear of Antinomianism among ministers, for the last few years, that I fear they have greatly neglected to hold up the real fulness and perfection of a present gospel-salvation. Many of them have been misled entirely by false statements that have been made in respect to Antinomianism, in the public journals which they take and read.

I have been astonished, as I have been abroad, to find how much misinformation was afloat in regard to the real views which we have here entertained and inculcated, and the results of exhibiting our views to this and other churches. This misinformation has led a great many ministers to feel it necessary to guard their people strongly against error in this direction. And in exposing what they have supposed to be the errors of Perfectionists and Sanctificationists, they have practically greatly lowered the standard of gospel holiness in their own churches. I mean this has been the practical result. Preaching against the doctrine of entire sanctification in this life, and holding out the idea, as many have, that Christians are expected to sin as long as they live—the practical result has been a perpetual backsliding on the part of their churches. Prejudice has been created against the doctrine of sanctification in the church; and, if I am not mistaken, ministers have greatly suffered in their own piety, in consequence of this course. And a consequent and corresponding descent in spirituality has been manifest in their churches.

I am fully persuaded that my brethren in the ministry will find it indispensable to insist on entire holiness of heart and life, as a practical attainment in this world, or they can never sustain a healthy piety in their churches.

My dear brethren, you may try it as long as you will; but if you take any lower ground than this, your churches will backslide until you yourselves will be appalled by the result. I am perfectly satisfied, from long experience, that there is no other way but to lodge the deep impression in the churches, that they are not only required, but expected to "cleanse themselves from all filthiness of the flesh and spirit, perfecting holiness in the fear of God." All pleading for sin, or anything that has the practical tendency of denying the practicability of attaining this state in this life, is the greatest and most ruinous error that can be inculcated on the churches. As said an English writer not long since: "No error is so destructive and to be so greatly denounced, as that Christians are expected to sin during this life."

My beloved brethren, in what I now say I am not endeavoring to win you to my opinion; but I wish to fix your attention and the attention of the church on the fact; and to have you witness the results of inculcating any lower practical standard than that which I have named.

The fact is, the churches are going rapidly away from God for want of the true bread of life; and because the ministry have, to such an alarming extent, been guarding their churches more against the doctrine of sanctification than they have against sin.

I beseech my brethren to adopt a different course, and urge the church right up to holy living, and let them know that they are expected to obey the law, and the gospel of God. Try it my brethren, and you will find it to be life from the dead to your churches. Do not be afraid of Antinomian perfectionism. It is not to me at all wonderful that at first, the true doctrine of sanctification and Antinomianism should be confounded in many minds, and that the defenders of the one should be confounded with the defenders of the other. But, beloved brethren, is it not time for ministers to understand as clear as sunlight the distinction between the two, and no longer be prejudiced or alarmed themselves, and no longer prejudice and alarm the church, by confounding things that so entirely differ?

I hope in what I now say, I shall not arouse the prejudice of my brethren so that they will not further hear me in what I have to say, in regard to the errors that have prevailed in the promotion of revivals of religion; and in regard to the causes that have operated to make them so few and far-between, and of so superficial a character.

My dear brethren, my heart is full of this subject and I have a great deal to say. I beg of you to hear me patiently and inquire honestly whether there has not been a great error in the direction that I have just named.

Your brother,

C. G. Finney

September 10, 1845

Dear Brethren:

Another thing that has acted very injuriously to the interests of revivals of religion is the false views that have prevailed in relation to the best means of promoting them. And in respect to means, if I have not been mistaken, there is a strong tendency to two opposite and almost equally injurious extremes. On the one hand, many seem to be expecting to promote revivals without the use of any special means whatever. Since revivals are the work of God, they think it enough to follow their ordinary sabbath exercises, with their regular weekly or monthly lectures, occasional prayer meetings, etc., and leave the event, as they say, with the sovereignty of God, believing these means to be sufficient, or that God can work just as well without any means whatever. They think it would be equivalent to taking the work out of the hand of God, and attempting to promote revivals in our own strength, to make any other efforts than the ordinary sabbath exercises, to promote the salvation of souls. Now, it appears to me that there is one principle of human nature here overlooked which must be regarded if we would successfully promote the kingdom of God. When any one mind or any number of minds are excited upon any topic, if you would gain their attention to any other subject, you must use means which are, in their nature, calculated to interest and excite them. Now the whole nominally Christian world is, and has been for the last thirty years, in a state of excitement, tending to a great moral revolution. By moral revolution, I mean, the revolution of opinion, and the consequent revolution of practice. Reform is the order of the day and many questions of deep interest are arising, one after another, to agitate the public mind, and the providence of God is pressing the whole mass of mind with agitating questions, and producing just about as much excitement as may be healthfully borne. These questions are political and religious; indeed there is scarcely any subject of deep and fundamental interest to mankind, that has not its advocates, lecturers, and public journals, through which it interests and excites the public mind. This excited state of mind is constantly increasing. Now it is perfectly unphilosophical to expect to so gain upon the attention of mankind, as to promote revivals of religion without making extra and protracted efforts. As the world is using steam-power to promote political agitation and reform, the ministry must "lift up their voices like a trumpet," "cry aloud, and spare not," and must multiply their efforts and their means in proportion to the excited state of the world on its topics, until, by the blessing of God, they gain the attention, and *keep* it, until the heart is subdued to God. It may be true that in those places where excitement upon other subjects but little prevails, revivals may be promoted without extra efforts, but if the church is expecting to promote revivals without great, powerful, and protracted efforts, they will find themselves mistaken. The fact that revivals are the work of God, instead of affording a reason for neglecting efforts, is the very reason which renders them indispensable. God does not subvert, but strictly adheres to the laws of mind in building up his kingdom and establishing his government in this world. For us, therefore, to plod on, and fear to use extra and exciting efforts to promote revivals of religion, while the world is all excitement on other subjects, is unphilosophical and absurd. It is true that great wisdom is needed to guard against indiscretion, and means of an *unnecessarily* agitating and exciting character, and means that will rather divert attention from the truth, than secure attention to the truth; but means must be used; meetings must be multiplied. Preachers and Christians must be themselves excited, and must be able to lift their voices above the winds and waves of this world's excitements, until they rivet attention, or they can never sanctify the heart. The erroneous view which stands opposed to this, and which seems to me to be an opposite extreme, I shall consider in a future letter.

Your brother,

C. G. Finney

October 22, 1845

Dear Brethren:

There is another class of Christians than those to whom I referred in my last letter, that seem to me to have fallen into an error opposed to that of which I then spoke. This class instead of taking the ground that no extra means are to be used for the conversion of sinners and the sanctification of the church, seem to have settled down in the belief that nothing can be done without protracted meetings, and the most exciting means that can be used. Hence they seem to be for doing up all their religious work in protracted meetings, giving up nearly their whole time to protracted effort, or a series of meetings, during a small part of each year, and make little or no effort to sustain the interests of religion, promote the conversion of sinners and the sanctification of the church, at other seasons.

Now it seems to me that this class of persons as radically misconceive the proper and only healthful method of promoting religion, as that class of Christians do to whom they stand opposed.

Now that a series of meetings, continued for days and weeks, may be useful, and in some instances demanded by the state of things, I think there can be no reasonable doubt. But as a general thing, it seems to me, that it would be more healthful for religion to have meetings for preaching, and prayer, and promoting the spirituality of Christians, so frequently, at all seasons of the year, as to secure the attention of the people, and yet so unfrequently as not to disturb their ordinary, or to say the least their necessary duties, in the relations which they sustain.

When I was first acquainted with revivals of religion, my own practice was this—and so far as I know it was the general practice of ministers and churches which endeavored to promote revivals of religion. We added to the services of the Sabbath as many meetings during the week as could well be attended, and yet allow the people to carry forward their necessary worldly business; and we went no farther than this. I have seen most powerful revivals of religion in the midst of harvest in a neighborhood of farmers, and found that it could be sustained by holding as many meetings as were consistent with farmer's securing their crops, and no more. The grand error which seems to me to have prevailed for the last few years, is this: Churches that are attempting to promote revivals, break in for a time on all the ordinary and necessary duties of domestic, commercial, agricultural and mechanical life; and make every day a Sabbath for a great number of days in succession, and then seem to be under the necessity of holding no meetings for a long time except on the Sabbath. They have neglected their worldly business so much and so long, that now they must make as much extra effort to bring up the arrears in that department, as they have made in their protracted meeting to bring up the arrears in the spiritual department. They go from one extreme to another, from holding meetings every day in the week, to holding meetings on which there is anything like a general attendance, no day in the week; from going to meeting nearly all the time until they have greatly neglected their worldly business, they break off and go to meeting at no time except on the Sabbath. Now it does seem to me that this is entirely unwise, and that its results are demonstrating to the churches, that the action of this course of things is not healthful, and that a better course would be to keep up as many meetings at all seasons of the year as can be sustained, and yet the necessary secular business transacted.

As excitement increases on other subjects, we shall find it necessary in the same proportion to increase the frequency and urgency of our appeals to mankind on the great subject of salvation. As I said in my last letter, if worldly men increase the means of exciting the people on worldly subjects, we must at least in equal porportion multiply the means for securing the attention of men to spiritual subjects. This seems to me to be a law of mind; and instead of this being set aside by the fact that revivals are produced by the Spirit of God, and instead of its being thereby rendered unnecessary to multiply means—inasmuch as means are essential to the Spirit's work, they must be multiplied if we expect divine influence to produce the desired result. Ministers have perceived with pain that through the instrumentality of protracted meetings the churches are taking on more and more the type of a spasmodic and temporary excitement on the subject of revivals, seizing on those seasons of the year when they have but little else to do, or neglecting whatever they have to do, and giving themselves up to a protracted effort, going to meetings day and night for a few days or weeks, and then relapsing to no effort. Whereas the churches should make a steady effort and put forth their energies every day, to secure the attention of people in proportion to the exciting topics on other subjects that are so pressed on them by worldly men, and worldly influences as to endanger their souls.

Your brother,

C. G. Finney

November 5, 1845

Dear Brethren:

Before I proceed farther on the subject of my last letter, I wish to call the attention of the brethren to an evil,
which seems to me to have greatly grieved the Spirit of
God, and to be at present a very effectual barrier to the
promotion of revivals of religion. I have already alluded
to it in a former letter, but wish more distinctly to dwell
on it here. The evil to which I allude is this—an amount
of prejudice has been excited against revival men and
measures, that has greatly grieved the Spirit of God. It
does not seem to me to have been sufficiently considered, that a mind under the influence of prejudice
cannot have communion with God, and consequently
cannot prevail in prayer, cannot appropriate the grace
that is essential to our living in such a manner as to
honor God. Now it cannot be denied that a course has
been taken that has filled the church throughout the
length and breadth of the land with a variety of prejudices that are eating out the piety of the churches and
preventing the promotion of revivals. Ministers have in
many instances, doubtless without designing such a
result, been instrumental in creating prejudices in the
minds of their churches, that have shut them out from
communion with God. They are in an uncandid state of
mind; they are committed and unwilling to hear with
both ears and then judge.

These prejudices extend to a great many subjects in
some churches. Great prejudices are excited against the
cause of abolition, moral reform, revival men and
measures, protracted meetings, New and Old School
Theology, sanctification, or anti-sanctification. Now it
matters little whether the prejudices are in favor of what
is really truth or against it. If they be really prejudices,
and the mind be committed and in an uncandid state it

effectually shuts the soul out from God. Prejudice is pre-judging a question. And pre-judgment is what Christ intended to prohibit and forbid. He did not design to teach that we should have no decided opinion, and form no unwavering judgment in respect to cases, questions, and characters on which we may be called to decide; but that we should not judge without a candid, thorough, and charitable examination in every case.

Now, ministers of a certain combative temperament are, without being aware of it, doing little else than preaching their people into the exercise of a host of prejudices that promote anything but their real piety. I have been shocked oftentimes on witnessing the prejudice evinced by ministers themselves, and by professors of all denominations.

Now, brethren, if we would promote revivals of religion among our people, we must fear to excite prejudices among them on any subject. They are naturally enough prone to prejudices—to rush into one sided judgments without our helping them into this ungodly state of mind by our preaching. If we come out and warn them against this thing, and that thing, and the other thing, denounce anti-slavery, moral reform, or even colonization, or anything else in a spirit and manner that creates prejudices, we may think ourselves doing God service, and may please ourselves when we behold our people very zealous for what we suppose to be truth; we may form and guard their orthodoxy until they have zeal enough to encompass sea and land to make proselytes to their opinions; and when we have done we shall perceive that they are only making their converts twofold more the children of hell than themselves.

Your brother,

C. G. Finney

Chapter V

HINDRANCES TO REVIVAL SPIRIT

Dear Brethren:

Another thing that is working an immense evil in the present day is the growing sectarianism of the church. It seems to me that the leading denominations that have heretofore been most zealous and successful in promoting revivals of religion, are within the last ten years becoming highly sectarian in their spirit and measures. The collision and sectarianism manifested by the former leading denominations, does not, I should think, increase in its degree or virulence, but these leading denominations are becoming divided amongst themselves, and seem to be very much given up to the spirit of schism and sectarianism. There is High Church and Low Church, Old School and New School, Reformers and Conservatives in all the denominations; and these seem to be pressing their peculiarities in a spirit, and by measures that are highly sectarian. Sectarian conventions, ecclesiastical meetings, councils, synods and all the parade and paraphernalia of sectarianism, seem to an alarming extent to be engrossing the mind of the Church.

Now this is certainly a great evil; and unless a counteracting influence can be brought to bear on the churches; unless ministers cease from this sectarian spirit—cease from these janglings and strife of words—cease from creating prejudices—cease from heresy-hunting, and all the management of ecclesiastical ambition, and give themselves up directly to promoting brotherly love, harmony in the church, the conversion of sinners and the sanctification of the saints, it is certain that revivals of religion cannot exist and go forward in purity and power.

What is peculiarly afflicting in view of this state of things is, that ministers and many Christians have become so thoroughly sectarian and are so thoroughly and deeply imbued with the spirit of sectarianism, as to be wholly unconscious that they are sectarian. They seem to suppose that it is a pure love of the truth, that they are only contending earnestly for the faith once delivered to the saints, that they are really and only jealous for the honor of God and the purity of the church. They have exalted their peculiar views in their own estimation, into fundamental doctrines, and contend for them with as much pertinacity and vehemence as if all must be reprobates who do not embrace them.

Now it is remarkable that so far as my knowledge extends, all the seasons of great revivals with which the church has been blessed from the very first, have been broken up and the revival influence set aside by an ecclesiastical and sectarian jangling, to preserve what they call the purity of the church and the faith once delivered to the saints. I believe it to be a truth, that ministers, as a class, have always been responsible for the decline of revivals; that their own sectarianism, ambition and prejudice have led them to preach and contend, to run to synods, councils, and other ecclesiastical meetings, until the churches, at first pained and even shocked with this tendency of things, have come to adopt their views, imbibe their spirit, and get entirely away from God.

My beloved brethren, who does not know that a vast many ministers are too much under the influence of prejudice to have communion and power with God? Who does not know that they are not sufficiently honest, uncommitted, upright, wholehearted lovers of truth to be thoroughly open to conviction on every subject, willing to examine patiently, and to judge charitably on every question on which they are to have or give an opinion? I have in my own experience learned that to maintain communion with God, I must wholly give up prejudice on every subject. I must hold my mind open to conviction; I must be thoroughly a candid and honest man. I must not allow myself to have or express an opinion on a subject that I have not carefully and prayerfully examined. There are many in these days that seem to have forgotten what God has said of those that "speak evil of things they understand not." And it is amazing to see to what an extent both ministers and professed Christians are given up to denouncing and speaking evil of things which they do not understand.

Now these ministers and Christians cannot pray. God will not hear them; they do not prevail with God, and everybody sees that they do not. They are not men that have power with God and with men and can prevail. They will denounce certain doctrines and certain things in a manner that is unutterably shocking to those who certainly know that they do not understand what they are talking about—who know that they are confounding things that radically differ, and making distinctions where there is no difference.

Now I might mention a great many facts and illustrations of this; but almost everyone is aware that it has been and still is perfectly common for ministers and private Christians to persist in confounding the views of entire sanctification which are entertained here with Antinomian Perfectionism. Now certainly those who do this, either do not mean what they say, or they have not well examined the subject. They are speaking what they do not know, and speaking evil of things that they understand not.

Now, my beloved brethren, I say not this to reproach anyone. But who does not know, after all, that this is true; or at least who *may* not know that it is true?

Now whether our peculiar views are true or false, it is wholly unfair to confound them with views which we abhor as much as they do.

Now if our views are untrue, let them be examined and stand or fall on their own merits. It may be convenient for those who oppose them to confound them with Antinomian Perfectionism or with Popery or with Universalism, or with any other *"ism"* that will attach to them so much opprobrium as to make the church unwilling ever to examine them for themselves. But let me say to my dear brethren, that whether our views are true or false, that way of disposing of them is certain to bring leanness into your own souls, and into the souls of your churches. And I ask of you, brethren, if it is not as a matter of fact producing this result? When you have been engaged in denouncing our views, or confounding them with Antinomianism, or persecuting them in ecclesiastical meetings, or in any way engaged in creating prejudices in opposition to them—I beseech you to consider, have you not found that this was bringing leanness into your own souls—that you were less spiritually-minded, had less communion with God, less heart to preach the gospel, less unction in preaching, and more and more of a sectarian spirit?

My beloved brethren, will you—ministers as well as laymen—candidly settle this question by laying open your heart at the throne of grace before the Lord?

Your brother,

C. G. Finney

December 3, 1845

Dear Brethren:

I designed to have prepared a letter for insertion previous to the one which appeared in the last paper, continuing my remarks on the subject of the use of means to promote revivals. I had said that there were two extremes, and that some were expecting to promote revivals only through the influence of protracted meetings and continuous efforts of that kind; while others were opposed to all such efforts. I also animadverted somewhat upon the tendency of certain Christians to compress nearly all their efforts for the promotion of religion into a few days and weeks of the year when they have little else to do, and do little or nothing for those objects at any other seasons of the year.

After I had finished that letter it occurred to me that it was liable to misapprehension, and as I said, I had designed to prepare the remarks which I now intend to make to follow that letter immediately. But as the one which appeared in your last was previously written, it has appeared without my fulfilling my intention.

The remarks which I now wish to make are summarily these:

1. All our time is God's.

2. All business is to be done for him.

3. Everything is to be done in its season. The Sabbath has its peculiar duties, and so has the spring, the summer, the autumn, and the winter. We are just as much required to labor six days as we are to rest on the Sabbath. In other words, all our time is to be devoted to God.

Now it often happens that in certain seasons of the year, most men have much more leisure than at other seasons—that is, God has much less for them to do with the ordinary labors in which he employs them. The farmer and indeed as a general thing all classes have less of the common business of life to transact in the winter than at other seasons of the year. Now it is highly reasonable and proper, and no doubt duty at such seasons to have our time all employed in something that shall promote the glory of God and the good of his kingdom. It is proper to hold more meetings, to labor more in prayer and visitation and in direct efforts for the conversion of sinners and the sanctification of Christians at such seasons than at other seasons when our duties to God plainly call us to till the ground, to gather the fruits of the field, or attend to any of the necessary business of life. To do all duties in their season affords no ground for the accusation that our religion is confined to protracted meetings, is a religion of the winter or of leisure days, etc. By itself this affords not a particle of evidence of a spasmodical and intermitting religion, any more than a man's going to church on the Sabbath, and working as God commands him to do through the week is evidence that his religion on the Sabbath is selfishness. The fact is a man may labor through the week for the same reason that he goes to meeting on the Sabbath—namely, to obey and glorify God. Nay, he must do this or he has no religion at all. He must be just as devout and just as much consecrated to God in his business as he is in going to meeting, or as he ought to be in going to meeting, or he has no religion at all.

So the farmer, merchant, or mechanic may be and is bound to be just as singly devoted to God—just as pious and holy in the labors of summer as in attending protracted meetings in the winter. The fact is, he is to do all for God, or in reality he does nothing for God. Unless he acts for the same end in the one case as in the other, and unless he acts in both cases with an eye single to the glory of God, he is not a holy man at all.

Now there is no certainty that a church is selfish because its members hold protracted meetings only at those seasons of the year when their duty to God, to their country, and to their families does not call them to other departments of labor. Whenever they can be spared from other departments of God's work, let them lay their hands to this. If they have any leisure time let them then make extraordinary efforts for the conversion of sinners and the sanctification of the church. This is reasonable—this is right, and I see not how this can be neglected without sin.

While then it is true and ought to be lamented that there is no doubt much spasmodical religion, or rather much that professes to be religion connected with and sometimes growing out of protracted meetings, yet it is by no means necessarily true that real Christians have turned aside from their duty in holding protracted meetings at some seasons of the year, and at other seasons of the year being very busy in laboring with their hands, tilling their grounds, plying their trades and serving God and their generation in their secular employments.

I wish therefore that it might be distinctly understood that it is very natural that revivals of religion should prevail at certain seasons of the year when the minds of both saints and sinners are less occupied with the necessary business of life. It is very natural and very important that special efforts should be made at such seasons, and that revivals of religion should be the result of such efforts.

It is therefore entirely out of place for the opposers of revivals and protracted meetings to object to them that they seldom occur except at those seasons of the year when people have comparatively little else to do. This is as might be expected. This is in a great measure as it should be. While therefore I would recommend, as I did in a former letter, that sufficient efforts should be made during all seasons of the year to keep religion alive in the hearts of Christians and to make aggressive movements upon the kingdom of darkness in the conversion of sinners, I would at the same time recommend and beseech my brethren to encourage the churches to make special and extraordinary efforts at every season of the year when time can be spared from other necessary avocations to attend more particularly to the great work of saving souls.

Your brother,

C. G. Finney

December 17, 1845

Dear Brethren:

In noticing the hindrances to revivals of religion I must not forget to urge more definitely and strongly than I have hitherto done, the great want of sympathy with Christ in the ministry and in the church. It cannot be expected and ought not to be, that the Spirit of God should be poured out and the labors of the church and the ministry be blessed in the salvation of souls any farther than there is a single eye, and a deep sympathy with Christ in the hearts of those who are forward as co-workers with him in the great work.

The Bible abundantly teaches that it is time for God to work and that the time to favor Zion has come, when the church "takes pleasure in her stones and favors the dust thereof." When the church and the ministry are deeply exercised with disinterested love to God and man—when they have such love for the brethren that they would die for them, and such love for precious souls as to be willing to toil and make any sacrifices, and even lay down life itself for their salvation—then, rely upon it, their labors will be blessed. And until they have this spirit they may indeed succeed in many instances in promoting an excitement and what they may call and may suppose to be a revival of religion; but ordinarily time will show that in truth it was no real revival of true religion.

When Christians and ministers are not in sympathy with God, they are not in a state to distinguish between spurious and genuine revivals of religion. Hence they often go forward with a series of efforts until many supposed converts are numbered, when in reality there is not a genuine convert among them. The reason is those who have been laboring in the work have begotten children in their own likeness. Not having the spirit of Christ themselves—not being deeply imbued with the true spirit of revival, they mistake their own excitement and the excitement around them for true religion, when it is perhaps anything else than a real work of the Holy Spirit. Now the more such efforts are multiplied, the more spurious conversions there are, so much the more are revivals brought into contempt and so much the more deeply the cause of Christ is injured.

Now I wish I could succeed in making the impression and fastening it not only on my own mind, but upon the minds of all the brethren that we cannot expect to succeed in promoting true revivals of religion any farther than we are truly revived ourselves—truly and deeply spiritual, having a general and all-absorbing sympathy with God—any farther than we are full of prayer and faith and love and the power of the Holy Ghost. There are so many kinds of excitement that are unfavorable to genuine religion, and yet so often mistaken for it that no man can safely engage in attempting to promote revivals of religion any farther than he truly and deeply communes with God and deeply enters into his sympathies. He must go forth and labor in the very spirit in which Christ came to die for sinners. He must have so single an eye that his whole body shall be full of light—that he will have deep spiritual discernment and be able in a moment in the light of God's Spirit shining in his own heart to detect every form and modification of spurious excitement. He wants to walk in such deep sympathy with God that his spirit will naturally repel every spirit that is not of God. There is, no doubt, such a state of mind as this.

But the thing which I wish more particularly to insist on in this letter is that the true revival spirit has been in a great measure grieved away from the church, and as far as my observation and knowledge extend, efforts to promote revivals of religion have become so mechanical, there is so much policy and machinery, so much dependence upon means and measures, so much of man and so little of God, that the character of revivals has greatly changed within the last few years, and the true spirit of revivals seems to be fast giving way before this legal, mechanical method of promoting them.

Now the thing that needs to be done is for everyone who would attempt to promote revivals of religion to be sure that he himself has a single eye, has a deep inward walk with God, has the life of God so richly developed within himself as to be able not only to prevail with God in prayer, but to preach the gospel to others with the Holy Ghost sent down from heaven, in demonstration of the Spirit and of power.

It would seem as if the ministry and the churches proposed to promote revivals in the hardness of their own hearts, and without deeply breaking up their own fallow ground. They get up protracted meetings and go to work to promote a revival without beginning first in their closets and thoroughly breaking down their hearts before the Lord, and getting all melted and subdued, filled with faith and with the Holy Ghost. They seem to expect that they shall get waked up during the meeting. They appoint a meeting while in a backslidden state, and of course in a selfish state of mind. They begin the meeting and perhaps continue day after day, the minister laboring for the conversion and waking up of the church while perhaps he himself is crusted over, hard-hearted, full of unbelief, worldly-mindedness, and with much respect to his own reputation as being deeply concerned in the progress of the work. Thus the meeting will continue day after day until they become considerably excited, have some confessions, and perhaps a few real conversions; but upon the whole, they have sowed among thorns instead of breaking up their fallow ground. Little else has been done perhaps than to produce discouragement and disgust in respect to revival efforts.

The fact is, brethren, a revival must take place among ministers. If there could be a protracted meeting for ministers—if some hundreds of ministers would assemble and preach and pray and labor for each other's spiritual welfare until there was a deep and thorough revival of religion among them—if they would deal so faithfully with each other and so affectionately as to get their hearts together, and together get into a deep sympathy with Christ, they would no doubt return from such a meeting to their several charges and the result would be a general revival of religion throughout their churches.

Brethren, what can be done to affect the ministry rightly, to bring them off from this jangling and sectarianism ambition and every evil way, and engage their hearts to live and die for Christ and for souls? Oh, this is the great thing needed. If this can be attained, the day of Zion's glory has dawned. But if ministers are to backslide and turn aside to vain jangling—to church politics and maneuvering, as they have for the last few years, I am persuaded that God must either let the churches under their influence go into a state of still deeper degradation and backsliding, or else he must set them aside and introduce some instrumentality independent of them to build up the wastes of Zion.

My soul is greatly troubled and my spirit is stirred

within me in looking at the state of the ministry.
Brethren, will you let me speak in love? Will you be offended with me if I tell you all my heart? For Zion's
sake, I cannot rest and for Jerusalem's sake I cannot
hold my peace. Will the brethren wake up and lay hold
on God for a general revival of religion? When shall it
once be?

Your brother,

C. G. Finney

January 7, 1846

Dear Brethren:

More than ten years since, I was led, I think by the
Spirit of the Lord, to perceive that the course of things
was tending rapidly towards the decline of revivals. Especially in this respect—there was very little of the right
kind of preaching to the Church, very little done and doing comparatively to elevate the standard of piety in the
churches and to promote their permanent spirituality.
Ministers, for the most part, were preaching and laboring directly for the conversion of sinners. This was the
order of the day. For a time God greatly prospered this
course; but as great multitudes of young converts were
introduced into the churches it was indispensable to the
continuance of a healthful state of piety that there
should be very much and very discriminating preaching
to the Church on the one hand, and every encouragement held out to make high attainments in spirituality
and deep piety on the other. I perceived that this was

greatly neglected by ministers in general, and that I had to some extent neglected it in my labors from church to church as an evangelist: for in this course of labor, my principal and in many instances my almost exclusive efforts were made for the conversion of sinners. I expected that ministers and old professors of religion would follow up these powerful revivals by a thorough course of training of young converts. But I saw that my expectations in this respect were by no means realized, and that consequently there was comparatively little growth in grace in the churches, and that their increase of spiritual strength and of aggressive power was by no means commensurate with their increase of numbers.

I believe it will be admitted by nearly all persons who are acquainted with the facts, that the converts in the revivals to which I allude have been to a great extent the strength and power of those churches from that time to this; and yet it is true that in those and in all other revivals of which I could hear, I perceived that they were not followed by that spiritual culture and training which promises to make the converts deeply spiritual and efficient Christians. The consequence has been that the converts in their turn set about the conversion of sinners with but a superficial piety of their own. Being untrained in deep spirituality and walking with God, and not being aware of the wiles of the devil, the Church to a great extent fell into a mechanical method of promoting revivals, which I could not but see would be attended with most disastrous consequences. Indeed I saw that the Church generally were getting into such a state that they would soon be wholly unable to promote true revivals of religion. I saw that they were losing the spirit of prayer and power with God, and that the tendency of things was to ruin revivals by substituting for them spurious forms of excitement.

Under this apprehension of things my own soul labored with great earnestness and agony for a deeper work in my own heart, that I might be able myself to exhibit more spiritual religion to the churches so far as I had access to them. When it pleased the Lord Jesus Christ to reveal himself more fully to my soul than he ever had done, and to show me heights and depths and lengths and breadths of the divine life which I never had perceived before, I was greatly impressed with the importance of elevating the standard of piety in the churches and of promoting among them a new type of religion in order to have them become so established in grace as to be kept from those temporary backslidings and effervescings that were disgracing religion.

But I can never reveal to man my astonishment and sorrow when I found that the ministry and the churches were so generally opposed to efforts to elevate the standard of piety among themselves. The cry was raised immediately—Why don't you preach to sinners? Why don't you labor for the conversion of sinners? Why are you endeavoring to reform the Church? I was astonished to find it generally assumed that the Church is well enough, and that the great and almost the only business of ministers is to promote the conversion of the ungodly.

Now I must say that this appeared to me then and has since to be a kind of spiritual infatuation. The state of the Church was fast becoming such as to render it a hopeless effort to aim at the real conversion of multitudes of the ungodly. The Church had been so little edified and built up in their most holy faith that they knew little or nothing of Christ except that he had died as an atoning sacrifice. Of the indwelling and energizing of his spirit within them—of holy walking and communion with Him—of being led by the Spirit—of denying all ungodliness and every worldly lust—of living above the world—of entire and universal consecration—of being filled with all the fullness of God: of these and such like things they were becoming to an alarming extent ignorant. Like people, like priest: the ministers to a great extent were in the same state. This I could not but perceive, and it filled me with unutterable agony.

I was not alone in these things. Here and there a brother in the ministry, and many in the churches throughout the length and breadth of the land I found had been led in the same way and had come to the same conclusions.

And now it does appear to me that the root of the difficulty that has arrested the onward, prosperous, and rising course of revivals of religion is that the *Church has been neglected.* It has been too much assumed that Christians would grow without food—would be established without spiritual culture—would honor God without deep, experimental piety. It seems to have been assumed that the Church would get along well enough if they could only add greatly to their numbers by the conversion of sinners. I have been deeply and unutterably grieved to find that efforts to reform the Church have been looked upon so coldly, and in many instances have been so deeply and bitterly opposed by multitudes of the Church and by great numbers of ministers. I have occasion to know that when the question has come up about my being invited to preach in certain churches, they have been willing that I should if I would preach to sinners, but they were not willing that I should preach to the Church. Once a written request was sent to me by a Presbyterian Church to come and preach a course of lectures to the impenitent. I have frequently heard of its being strongly objected to by ministers and leading church members that I should come and preach to Christians. They were unwilling to have Christians reproved and searched, and deeply overhauled to the very foundations of their hope. I have often heard fault found with that course of preaching which shakes the hopes of professors of religion. This kind of preaching has been spoken of again and again as so very objectionable that it was not to be tolerated.

Now when the ministers will take such a course as this, where will their people appear in the day of judgment? What! afraid to be searched, and to have their churches searched! afraid to have the broadest daylight of truth poured in upon them? "Oh," said one minister, as I was informed, when requested to invite me to come and labor with his people, "I should like to have him come if he would confine his preaching to the impenitent, but I cannot bear to have him rake the Church."

Now, beloved brethren, I have heard much complaint of the attempts that have been made within the last ten years to revive religion in the churches, and to elevate the standard of piety among them. And is it really to this day assumed that the churches do not need reformation? Well, all I can say to my dear brethren is this: You maintain this stand but a little longer, and it does not need a prophet's ken to predict that your churches will be anything but Christian Churches. That they are even now tending rapidly to a high church spirit is but too manifest. Can it be possible that after all the developments that have been made, any of the brethren should be so blind as not to see that a blow must be struck at the foundation. The ax must be laid at the root of every barren fig tree. Ministers must turn their attention to digging about and manuring these trees. An effort must be made to search, revive and purify the churches. Old professors and the converts of the recent revivals must be searched and overhauled; their foundations examined and their hearts entirely reclaimed. They must be built up and spiritualized and established in grace so as to be living epistles of Christ known and read of all men, or to attempt the farther promotion of revivals of religion is vain and worse than vain.

The fact is, brethren, that the resistance that has been offered to labors for the reformation of the Church has deeply grieved the Spirit of God. The ministry and the Church have to a great extent refused to be searched. They have refused to be reformed, and the result is that the Spirit of God has left and is fast leaving them.

If I should say less than this, I should not speak the whole truth; but in saying so much I am not without my fears that I shall offend some of my brethren. Dear brethren, I beg of you not to be offended with me but suffer me to speak the whole truth to you in love. Is it not true with many of you who are ministers as well as laymen that you have refused candidly to lay your mind open to reproof, to correction, to searching, and to the light of the whole gospel of Christ? Is it not true that you have resisted the reformation of your own heart, and the efforts that have been made to revive the Church and to elevate the standard of holiness within her borders? Have you not been more afraid of sanctification than you have of sin, and have you not resisted efforts that have been made to enlighten you and the churches over which you preside? May God help you, my brother, to be honest in answering these questions. Have you not in many instances not only shut your own eyes against the light, but tried to keep the light from the eyes of others? Have you not refused to read what has been written on the subject of holiness in this life, and used an influence to prevent others from reading? Have you not even spoken against this subject, and spoken contemptuously of those whose hearts are laboring and agonizing and travailing in birth for the recovery of a backsliding Church?

My brethren, these are plain questions; they are intended to be. Could I see you, I could ask you these questions on my knees; and would it avail, I would wash your feet with my tears. My brethren, where are you, and where are your churches? What is your spiritual state? How stands the thermometer of your spirituality? Are you hot or cold or lukewarm? Are you agonizing to elevate the standard of holiness in the Church, and in your own heart; or are you still assuming that the Church is well enough, and looking coldly and contemptuously upon all efforts to revive her?

May the Lord have mercy on us, my brethren, and search us all out, and compel us to come to the light, to confess our sins and put them all away forever, and lay hold on the fullness there is in Christ.

Your brother,

C. G. Finney

Chapter VI

THE ATTITUDE OF THE CHURCH

Dear Brethren:

There is one subject upon which I must remark further, and yet I fear it will be impossible to do it justice without giving offence. One of the most serious impediments that have been thrown in the way of revivals of religion and one that has no doubt deeply grieved the Spirit of God is the fact that the church to a very great extent has lost sight of its own appropriate work and has actually left it in a great measure to be conducted by those who are for the most part illy prepared for the work. The work to which I allude is the reformation of mankind.

It is melancholy and amazing to see to what an extent the church treats the different branches of reform either with indifference, or with direct opposition. There is not, I venture to say upon the whole earth an inconsistency more monstrous, more God-dishonoring and I must say more manifestly insane than the attitude which many of the churches take in respect to nearly every branch of reform which is needed among mankind.

To such an extent is this true that scarcely a church can be found in the land which as a body will have anything to do with reform. Hence the only way in which Christians in the churches who would do anything towards reforming mankind can make their influence felt is by forming societies, composed often partly of Christians and partly of those who profess no religion. These unite together to concentrate their influence against some form of iniquity that is cursing mankind.

Now the great business of the church is to reform the world—to put away every kind of sin. The church of Christ was originally organized to be a body of reformers. The very profession of Christianity implies the profession and virtually an oath to do all that can be done for the universal reformation of the world. The Christian church was designed to make aggressive movements in every direction—to lift up her voice and put forth her energies against iniquity in high and low places—to reform individuals, communities, and governments, and never rest until the kingdom and the greatness of the kingdom under the whole heaven shall be given to the people of the saints of the most High God—until every form of iniquity shall be driven from the earth.

Now when we consider the appropriate business of the church—the very end for which she is organized and for which every Christian vows eternal consecration, and then behold her appalling inconsistencies everywhere apparent, I do not wonder that so many persons are led to avow the solemn conviction that the nominal church is apostate from God. When we consider the manner in which the movement in behalf of the slave has been treated by ecclesiastical bodies, by missionary associations, by churches and ministers, throughout the land, is it any wonder that the Church is forsaken of the Spirit of God?

Look at the Moral Reform movement. A few devoted self-denying females, engaged in a mighty conflict with the great sin of licentiousness. This struggle has been maintained for years; and yet how few comparatively of the churches as such have treated this effort in any other way than with contempt? A few devoted Christian women in various churches form societies to aid in this work; but where are the churches themselves as a body? Where are these sworn reformers—these men and women who profess to be waging everlasting war against every form of sin? Where are the ministry? Do they lift up their voice like a trumpet? Do they cry aloud and spare not? Do they, as John Adams says, thunder and lighten from their pulpit every Sabbath against these sins?

It is amazing to see what excuses are made by ministers for remaining silent in respect to almost every branch of reform.

And pray, what can be meant by the sickening cry of moral suasion? The Church with a great many ministers have resorted to the plea of using moral suasion as the means of ridding the world of intemperance, licentiousness, slavery and every other legalized abomination; but pray what can be meant by moral suasion? Moral government surely is a system of moral suasion. Moral suasion includes whatever is designed and adapted to influence the will of a moral agent.

Law, rewards, and punishments—these things and such as these are the very heart and soul of moral suasion. It would seem as if a great many people mean by moral suasion nothing more than flattery and palaver. Consequently when efforts are made to secure legislation that shall put these abominations away, they are afraid to employ government lest it would be a departure from the system of moral suasion. But is not God's government one of moral suasion? Are not his mighty judgments on the one hand and his mercies on the other, moral suasion?

But not to dwell on the subject of moral suasion; the idea I wish to present to the brethren is this—the great sin and utter shame of the Church and of so many of the ministry in neglecting or refusing to speak out and act promptly and efficiently on these great questions of reform. How could they more directly grieve and quench the Spirit of God than by such a course? Abandon the great work to which they are pledged and sworn, and yet profess to be Christians! No wonder that such a church and such a ministry should look coldly on revivals and find it impossible to promote them. After so much light has blazed before the churches on these subjects, it cannot be that they resist or neglect without great sin.

And shall it be persevered in? If so there can be no

doubt that revivals must utterly cease—that the Spirit of God will be grieved entirely away from the ministry and the churches, and nothing better can be expected than utter and universal desolation.

Believe me, dear brethren, it grieves me greatly to feel constrained to speak thus. Is it not a shame; are we not ashamed and shall we not blush to see the Church of God not only turn back from reforming the world—refusing to lead in reform as she ought to do, and then turn round and oppose others who are compelled to lead for want of the help and countenance of those who ought to go forward in these enterprises? If doctors of divinity—if ecclesiastical bodies, theological seminaries and colleges would but lead on in these enterprises, God forbid that they should not have their place. If they would but go forward the Church would follow them, and many who are now compelled to lead because these refuse, would rejoice to fall in behind and sustain them with all their might.

But if the church will not lead—if doctors of divinity, ecclesiastical bodies, colleges and seminaries will do nothing but get together to pass resolutions condemning the movements of reform, what shall be done? Shall they refuse to work in these departments and also hinder those who would work? Who pretends that so great wisdom has been manifested in the various branches of reform as might have been, had the Church with her spiritual leaders only taken the right position? What can be expected but error and confusion, while nearly all the spiritual influence in the world is brought to oppose instead of promote reforms? My brethren, if ecclesiastical bodies, colleges and seminaries will only go forward, who will not bid them Godspeed? But if they will not go forward—if we hear little or nothing from them but complaint, denunciation, and rebuke in respect to almost every branch of reform, what can be done?

My soul is sick and agonized with such a state of

things. The position of the Church is one of the greatest wonders of the world—and yet we are gravely asking, why we do not have revivals of religion? Why has the Spirit of God forsaken us? and many are even glad to have revivals cease, and seem disposed to quell everything down into a state of death-like apathy on every branch of reform.

Now until the Church shall arise and take a different attitude, I am confident that nothing else can be expected than a retrograde movement on the part of the Churches until not even a form of godliness remains among them.

Why cannot we all do in respect to reforms as Pres. Edwards did in respect to revivals? He fearlessly pointed out whatever was wrong and of evil tendency in the means used to promote them, and at the same time was careful to show a more excellent way. His opposition to what was wrong, although fearless and uncompromising, was never so prominent as to overshadow all his engagedness in promoting them. He was their powerful, zealous, and successful advocate and promoter. It became him then to speak out and rebuke whatever was wrong. Everybody saw that his rebukes arose not from opposition to revivals as such, but from his great love for them and from a quenchless zeal to promote them. When he lifted his admonitory voice, the friends of revivals would listen because they knew it to be the voice of a friend and not of an enemy of revivals. Everybody knew he spake of the evils sometimes connected with revivals because he loved them in their purity.

Now why cannot we all do so on the subject of reform? My brethren, let us all come forward and show ourselves to be reformers—put our heads and hearts together to promote every branch of reform and also revivals of religion, and then we shall hold a position in which we can successfully oppose and correct the errors of the day either in revivals or reforms. But who will

listen to ministers, ecclesiastical bodies, doctors of
divinity, missionary societies, or anybody else who make
no aggressive movements at all in respect to any reform and say almost nothing except to rebuke and con-
demn? They can talk eloquently of the evils incident to
revivals, but are not like Pres. Edwards, zealous and
successful in promoting them themselves. They can
denounce the madness of abolitionists and the errors
and extravagances of both the leaders and followers in
other reforms; but alas, how few of them have anything
efficient or impressive to say to promote these great objects either by encouragement, instruction or counsel.

Now if ecclesiastical bodies generally, doctors of
divinity, colleges and theological seminaries, had uniformly manifested zeal in all departments of reform, they
would be heard. If ministers had manifested zeal and efficiency in these reforms, their churches would hear and
respect them, and the ministry might lead them
anywhere. But now the ministers are complaining that
their churches are divided—that they themselves are
losing the confidence of their people—that ministerial
influence is becoming paralyzed—and church influence
an abomination.

Is it possible, my dearly beloved brethren, that we
can remain blind to the tendencies of things—to the
causes that are operating to produce alienation, division,
distrust, to grieve away the Spirit, overthrow revivals,
and cover the land with darkness and the shadow of
death? Is it not time for us, brethren, to repent, to be
candid and search out wherein we have been wrong and
publicly and privately confess it, and pass public resolutions in our general ecclesiastical bodies, recanting and
confessing what has been wrong—confessing in our
pulpits, through the press, and in every proper way our
sins as Christians and as ministers—our want of sympathy with Christ, our want of compassion for the slave,

for the inebriate, for the wretched prostitute, and for all the miserable and ignorant of earth?

May the Lord have mercy on us, my brethren.

Your brother,

C. G. Finney

February 4, 1846

Dear Brethren:

Another subject upon which I wish to address my brethren has respect to an error, which I fear is greatly interfering with the progress of revivals. I mean the fears that are so generally entertained respecting religious excitement, and indeed excitements on any branch of reform. Many seem to dread excitements greatly, and to be rather guarding against them than laboring to promote revivals of religion.

I have before said something upon the subject of excitement; but I am continually becoming more and more acquainted with the extent to which these fears of excitement prevail, and the great consequent evils. Many ministers seem to be so much afraid lest religious excitement should be spurious, and are guarding so strongly against spurious excitement that they really prevent all excitement.

Now it seems to me that few things can be more directly calculated to put down a revival should it commence, or to keep it down and prevent its even commencing, than to be continually guarding the people against false excitements, pointing out the marks of spurious excitements and turning the mind away from the great truths of the gospel by which men are to be sanctified, to consider those spurious forms of excitement that have often cursed the world. The fact is that spurious excitements almost always result from preaching error. Preaching truth, the whole truth, and nothing but the truth, and especially those great and fundamental truths that are indispensable to salvation, keeping clear of all admixture of error and fanaticism, either in the doctrine taught, or in the spirit of preaching, tends in the highest degree to beget a wholesome excitement, and no other than this. To arouse the attention strongly, and fix it upon those truths in their soundness and power, is the most ready way to prevent all spurious excitements and to promote those which are sound, healthful, and evangelical. Whereas to neglect to preach this class of truths, and devote one's self to guarding the people against spurious excitement is almost sure, either wholly to allay all excitement or to arouse the combativeness of any who may have begun to drink in a spirit of spurious excitement, and drive them still farther from the truth.

The fact is, my dear brethren, a great many ministers and churches appear to be too much afraid of spurious excitements to use any thorough means to promote revivals. They are afraid to make a powerful appeal—are afraid to lift up their voice like a trumpet, and blow a blast long and loud in the ears of the people, and to press them with overcoming urgency to lay hold on eternal life, lest they should promote a spurious excitement. If at any time an excitement commences in the church, manifesting itself in prayer and conference meetings, forthwith some over prudent elder, deacon or minister begins to throw out cautions against spurious excitements. Now this is the very way to render revivals impossible. The proper way is to guard against all those doctrines and measures that are calculated to inflame the imagination and stir up an ocean of excitement, without informing the intelligence; and to press most importunately, frequently, and powerfully the real truths of the gospel—those truths which sinners and professed saints most need to know, and if possible, to rivet and hold them so thoroughly to those truths as to afford no room for fanaticism, in doctrine or feeling, to get a footing. Then if at any time suspicious things appear, the best of all ways to correct them, so far as my experience goes, is, when it can be done, to labor in private with the individuals who are under the false excitements, and if it can possibly be avoided, not to divert the congregation by preaching upon the subject. Let the congregation be held fast by the great truths that are adapted to break their hearts, and if a dash of fanaticism or enthusiasm appears now and then, I would advise by all means, as I have said in a former letter that private interviews should correct these evils without letting the congregation know that any notice has been taken of them.

The thing I am recommending, is by no means to aim at promoting great excitement. But it should be remembered that great revivals of religion can never exist without deep excitement of feeling; and yet it is the revival of religion at which we ought to aim; and since some excitement is naturally and necessarily incidental to a revival of religion, let it come and do not fear it. Do let us remember and believe my brethren, that the readiest of all ways to prevent enthusiasm, fanaticism, and spurious excitements, is to thunder forth with power and in demonstration of the Spirit the solid and fundamental truths of the gospel, both in season and out of season.

One thing I wish to press especially upon the brethren: *The people will be excited*; and they will be excited on the subject of religion. If you keep out that wholesome excitement which the naked and sound gospel is adapted to promote, you may rest assured that sooner or later, spurious excitements, or excitements that you cannot control will spring up among your people, and will distract and carry them away as with a flood. Brethren, this is no age of the world for us to dream that we can keep the churches from excitement. They cannot be kept from it, and they ought not to be. The indications of providence are plain and palpable that the excitements now abroad in the land are not to cease. Every turn in Divine Providence only multiplies the occasions and the means of excitement, and it is madness for us to throw ourselves in the way of Divine Providence, and suppose that we can correct this railroad movement of the public mind. Our inquiry should be: how shall we guide it? How shall we so control and promote it as to prevent evil and secure good results? How shall we direct and keep it within its proper channels? To attempt to arrest it were as idle as to attempt to cut off the waters of the Mississippi. Dam it across in one place, it will break out and flow in another. If we don't keep those mighty currents of excited mind in their proper channel, they will desolate the whole land. Who does not see that if we succeed in arresting excitement on one subject, immediately the waters swell and break out in another direction. Another and another subject comes up and keeps the public mind in perpetual fermentation. Who can prevent it? No man; and it ought not to be prevented. If ministers and professed Christians instead of taking advantage of the present state of things, and making clear the proper channel and guiding the public mind right by a powerful exhibition of the gospel—if instead of this, they will attempt to arrest all excitement, they must expect their people to become divided; factions and excitements will spring up; anarchy and misrule will prevail, until ministers—the shepherds of the flock—have lost their influence, and error and fanaticism carry away the public mind.

Brethren, we have the means in our hand of guiding the public mind—of molding or modifying the excitements that overspread the land. Let ministers and Christians take their station beside the pool of life, and lift their voices above the winds and waves of popular excitement and cry, "Ho, every one that thirsteth, come ye to the waters, and he that hath no money come; yea come, buy wine and milk without money and without price." Instead of being afraid of spurious excitement, with the experience and the means that we have, it seems to me to be certain, that the church can go forward in the promotion of revivals, until the whole land and the whole world are subdued to Christ, without the introduction and prevalence of one spurious religious excitement.

The gospel is adapted to promote a healthful excitement. Let us throw it out upon the people in all its length and breadth and power. Then, whatever excitement is incidental to such a procedure, let it come. Let ministers and Christians be sober-minded and hold fast to the truth and to the form of sound words, and use those measures and those only, which are needed and are most adapted to secure a universal attention to the truth, and bring about as speedily and universally as possible a thorough submission to God. My brethren, do not let us stand timidly by, and criticize and warn against false excitements, and hush everything down and keep our people asleep, till ere we are aware, they break loose from our influence and run headlong and in masses after some fanatical leader to the ruin of their souls.

Your brother,

C. G. Finney

February 18, 1846

Dear Brethren:

Another subject on which I wish to address my brethren, is a tendency which I perceive to exist in the public mind towards a conclusion which to me appears little short of downright infatuation, namely, that the churches can exist and prosper as well without revivals of religion as with them, or even better. Now this is certainly the most preposterous conclusion conceivable; and yet I really know not what else to infer from the general apathy upon the subject of revivals, and especially from the quite extensive hostility against them which is apparent in many sections of the church. Many of the leading men in the church seem about ready to adopt, or at least are earnestly favoring the policy of making no efforts to promote revivals—of discountenancing the labors of evangelists, and all those extra means and efforts that have been used from time immemorial, whenever revivals have occurred.

Now, that the Christian church cannot exist without extensive revivals of religion can be clearly demonstrated; unless the Lord introduces a different mode of diffusing the gospel, from any that He ever has adopted. Nay, indeed, the very supposition is absurd and self-contradictory. What! Can it be conceived that the church can succeed in converting the world without revivals? Must not the church herself be revived? Must not religion be revived among the impenitent? If not, will not true piety well nigh cease from the world? The nominal church might exist, I grant, without revivals. They might introduce another half-way covenant system, or receive hosts of ungodly men to the church without their giving any evidence of regeneration; and thus a nominal church might be kept up; but that true piety cannot exist and spread without a great and general revival of religion, and without revivals succeeding declensions as often as declensions in any portions of the church shall occur, is to my mind one of the plainest truths in the world.

I am sorry that I have not the means by me of stating definitely the real results of those experiments that have been tried of promoting religion without revivals; but who does not know that in such cases, the churches have either become extinct, or have become merely nominal churches, having only a name to live while really dead. They have resorted to a half-way covenant, and various other means of filling up the church from the world, without their being truly converted to God. How else could even the nominal church exist? Christians continue to die, and die in fact much faster than sinners will be converted to fill their places without revivals. I believe it to have been a universal fact that church members have died faster than sinners have been converted to fill their places where no means have been used to promote revivals, and where consequently they have not existed. But it is the consummation of folly for the church to expect to keep pace at all with the rapid increase of the earth's population and especially with the increase of population in this country, without very extensive, continuous and pure revivals. Revivals alone can secure the stability and perpetuity of our religious and civil institutions. I do not believe that this government could exist in its present form, fifty years without revivals; nor is it at all likely to me that it would exist half that time. It was remarkable to see to what an extent the revivals in this country from 1820 to 1840 influenced the public mind, developed reforms, and brought up as from the depths of oblivion the great truths and principles that are the sheet-anchor of every government of opinion under heaven. The fact is, those revivals affected all classes of the community. They affected the whole country and have extended their influence throughout all Christendom. This I have very good reason to know, not only from my acquaintance with this country, but from abundant intelligence received from Europe.

These revivals were beginning and indeed more than beginning to influence the legislation of all Christendom. But let them be done away—let the generation that has witnessed their power go to their graves without the recurrence of those scenes, and what will be the result? A government of mere opinion like ours, in the hands of a people who fear not God, with a temporizing ministry, a licentious press, and all the agencies that are at work to carry headlong all the religious institutions of the land—where are we in twenty or in fifty years without revivals of religion? Witness the efforts of the papacy—the tendencies of Puseyism—the efforts of Universalists and errorists of every description—the running to and fro of lecturers on every subject—the spread of infidel books and tracts, and all the enginery of hell to overthrow all order and law and everything that is lovely and of good report; and then say, my brethren, can the church exist and prosper without revivals of religion?

But to come nearer home—can we or the present church become anything less than an abomination and a curse to the world without revivals? Whither is she tending already? Witness the gossip, the worldliness, the pride, the ambition—everything that is hateful— growing up and prevailing in churches, just in proportion as they are destitute of the reviving influences of the Holy Spirit. Contemplate the cowardice, the trimming policy, the ecclesiastical ambition of the ministry without revivals of religion—mark how great and overcoming are their temptations to please men and even ungodly church members, when there are no copious outpourings of the Spirit to arouse the multitude and strengthen the hands of the servants of God.

Oh, it is impossible that desolation should not reign—that the ministry should not cower down before an ungodly public sentiment—that Popery should not prevail, the Sabbath be desecrated—the church ruined and the world undone, without great revivals of religion.

And what can this policy mean, that would hush everything down and frown on all special efforts to promote revivals? It is certainly infatuation, and if not arrested, it must end in ruin.

I beseech my brethren in the name of our Lord Jesus Christ to keep as far as possible from the appearance or the thought of discountenancing or looking coldly on revival efforts. They are our life. They are the salvation of the church—they are the hope of the world. Instead of allowing them to cease, every minister and Christian ought to aim at increasing them a hundred fold. Every one of us ought to set his heart upon rendering them pure, deep, universal, and as frequent as the necessities of the church and the world demand. Let no man stop short of aiming at this as he values his own soul, and the souls of his fellowmen.

Your brother,

C. G. Finney

April 29, 1846

Dear Brethren:

If I am not mistaken, the churches have fallen into an error in many cases, in respect to the course which it is incumbent on them to take when an evangelist leaves the grounds. When one has been employed, and his labors have been greatly blessed, and the time comes for him to leave and take another field, it is then peculiarly important that the church should rally to a man, sustain their pastor, sustain all the meetings, and make more vigorous exertions than ever to push forward the work. But it happens in some instances, instead of taking this course, they seem to regard the leaving of the evangelist as a signal for them to indulge unbelief, retire from the work, cease to labor and visit and pray, neglect meetings, and in short to take the very course that is in the highest degree calculated to discourage the pastor, to grieve the Spirit of God, and to bring on a reaction inevitably, and most dangerous results in various ways.

Again, the churches have often fallen into an error in respect to what was to be expected of the pastor, and in respect to the state of things when the evangelist leaves the grounds. It often happens that the evangelist remains on the grounds as long as the excitability of the congregation continues in such strength that the work can be pushed with unabated power. He remains until perhaps the church, especially those members who have labored most efficiently together with the pastor—and indeed, until the mass of mind is brought into a state so nearly bordering on exhaustion, that from the very laws of mind, there must necessarily be a pause, or at least a temporary suspension of the power of the excitement.

Now when the evangelist leaves the grounds, especially if he has remained until the circumstances are such as I have just supposed, it is generally to be expected that the work will take on a somewhat and oftentimes a materially different type—that the power of the excitement will more or less abate, and perhaps many persons who have attended the meetings more from curiosity than from any heart-interest in them, will relinquish their attendance; there will naturally be a falling off of numbers, of excitement, and many of the circumstances will tend to discourage both the pastor and the church.

Now just in these circumstances churches should be very considerate, and not suffer unbelief on the one hand to prevail, or a censorious, faultfinding spirit to come in on the other. This change of appearance ought not to discourage the expectation of Christians that the work will go on, although under a modified type.

But right here an evil of this kind is sometimes observable. The evangelist has left the grounds, a change, more or less, has come over the community—and the church often suffer their hearts to go off with the evangelist, their faith to fail with respect to the continuance of the work among them, and soon it begins to be thought, and of course to be spoken of among the brethren, that the pastor cannot sustain the work; they begin to find fault with him, instead of sustaining him by prayer and every means of encouragement within their reach. Instead of putting forth their utmost exertions to help him just at this critical point, they cruelly abandon him and the work, and gradually give themselves up to faultfinding, until finally the pastor is discouraged, the Holy Spirit is grieved—the pastor's feelings are thrown into such an attitude that he has not courage and strength to feed and lead forward the converts—a disastrous reaction comes over the community, and shortly it is agreed on all hands that it is best to have a change of ministers. Now somewhat in this way, if I am not mistaken, not a few pastors have been induced to leave their flocks soon after most powerful and glorious revivals.

Now in these cases there is utterly a fault somewhere. Both the church and the pastor may be to blame. And sometimes it is to be found that the evangelist himself has not taken pains enough before his leaving, to guard the church against such a course and such results. It is of the utmost importance that the evangelist himself should understand and fully appreciate the frailty of Christians in this respect, their great liability to err, the circumstances of temptation under which they will be placed, and the evil that will inevitably result if those things should accrue of which I have spoken. The evangelist ought deeply to feel that if his influence disturbs the pastoral relation—nay, if it does not strengthen and establish pastoral influence; if he does not encourage instead of discourage the pastor; if he does not do him good instead of evil, his labors are not what they ought to be as an evangelist, and what they must be to be long sustained and desired by the churches. Notwithstanding all these dangers, if the church are but instructed and on their guard, do they but know and feel what they ought to know and feel in respect to their relations and duties to each other, to their pastor, to the evangelist, and to the great work in which they are engaged—do but the evangelist and the pastor know and do their duty, understand their relations to each other, to the church, and to their great work, glorious results may most reasonably be expected from the employment of evangelists in the promotion of revivals.

But from what has been said, it is very easy to see that an evangelist needs to be pre-eminently a wise man to manage wisely and prudently under the ever-varying circumstances in which he will find himself placed. So to demean himself as to leave a healthful influence in the churches where he labors, requires an uncommon degree of wisdom. Few men comparatively are qualified for this office. I have repeatedly known young men to get the impression that it was their duty to be evangelists, who would labor in that capacity but a short time, and for want of wisdom and those peculiar characteristics that are indispensable to the success of an evangelist, would find themselves hedged in as evangelists, and such a lack of order in the churches as to find it difficult to procure such a settlement as otherwise they might have procured.

By these remarks I do not design to discourage young men from becoming evangelists if they are qualified for this arduous and peculiar work.

Your brother,

C. G. Finney

Chapter VII

THE IMPORTANCE OF EVANGELISTS AND LAYMEN

Dear Brethren:

In connection with this subject I wish to say to my brethren several things in regard to employing evangelists in promoting revivals.

And here I suppose I need not say that such a class of ministers is distinctly recognized in the Bible, and that they are manifestly in some sense itinerating ministers of the gospel, and distinguished from pastors particularly in this—that they had no stated charge or particular church or congregation over which they presided. They seem to have been employed by the Holy Ghost to travel among the churches and perform that kind of labor to which they were adapted, and which their relations rendered it peculiarly proper for them to perform. I design to say more in detail upon this subject hereafter.

And further I suppose I need not attempt to show that in every age of the Christian church—to say nothing of the older dispensation, whenever religion has been extensively revived, the employment of evangelists, or what has been equivalent to this, has uniformly been resorted to by the Holy Spirit in promoting the work. I am not aware that any extensive revival has ever existed without the use of this particular means in connection with other means for its promotion. Sometimes evangelists, properly so called, have been employed; at other times laymen and pastors have gone abroad, visiting and laboring with the churches. I think it cannot be denied that one of the most efficient influences ever used by the Holy Spirit in promoting revivals is some form of itinerant labor either of ministers or of laymen.

The things however which I wish to say do not so much respect the validity and importance of the office and labors of evangelists as the mistakes into which the churches have fallen respecting them—mistakes which have led to extensive prejudices against their labors.

And first I should observe that plainly there are comparatively few men well qualified for evangelists. An evangelist needs very peculiar characteristics, without which they will almost inevitably work mischief in the churches. Without these peculiar qualifications, they may indeed do some and even much good; but they will be apt to disturb the relation of the pastors so seriously and get up such a state of things in the churches as will tend ultimately and necessarily to their own expulsion from those churches.

Some of the things which I wish to say upon the subject are the following.

1. An evangelist should be an *unambitious man.* If he is ambitious, he will inevitably not only grieve the Spirit of God, but will aim to gather about himself an influence and a power, and if in the providence of God he should acquire it, he will use it in such a manner as to embarrass and distract rather than edify the church of God.

2. He should be a man of meekness. It is natural that he should meet with very much opposition. Unless he is a man of good temper, and of great meekness, bearing with patience and without retort the many things that may be said and written against him, he will inevitably excite angry disputes and divisions rather than promote godly edification.

3. He should be a man of discretion, so as not to be guilty of rashness in any of his movements. He should especially avoid any such rashness as might justly array the influence of pastors against himself.

4. He should be very careful not to break open the door and enter fields of labor which the Lord has not prepared for him. When evangelists are abroad and revivals occur under their labors, there is in almost every church more or less men and women who are perhaps

really pious people, but withal a little headstrong and indiscreet, who are for crowding their measures and insisting upon having evangelists come and labor in their churches, before either their pastors or the body of the church are at all prepared for such a movement.

I said it is almost inevitable that an evangelist should have many things said against him. Many reports will be circulated, prejudical to his influence and labors. These will come to the ears of pastors and churches, who may not have the means, and possibly not the heart to search into and find out the truth upon these points. Consequently they are by no means prepared to receive the evangelist. Yet if he be a discreet and holy man—if his labors are truly useful, this will be known, and the knowledge will extend fast enough to open the eyes and the hearts of ministers and people to receive him into different fields as fast as he is able to occupy them.

Now the thing I wish to say right here is this—that if a man has not discretion enough to refrain from pushing his labors into places, congregations and neighborhoods, where Christian churches exist and where the ministers are good men and yet by no means prepared to receive him—he will soon hedge himself in round about and be generally resisted by the pastors and churches. If he will patiently labor from field to field as God throws the door wide open before him, it appears to me certain that prejudice will give way quite as fast as he is able to go forward and occupy the opening fields of labor. But if on account of the importance of particular places he listens to the invitation of a few who are urgent to have him come, while the ministry and churches in general, and especially the minister and many of the very church to which he is invited are through prejudice or misapprehension entirely unprepared to receive him, there may in such a case be some revival, but there will be much distraction and ultimately a powerful reaction. Indeed few things are a more sore trial to pastors than to have a few zealous men in their churches overrule their own judgments and call in to labor in the congregation an evangelist of whose labors they sincerely stand in doubt. They sometimes yield to this as the least of two evils.

But I would most seriously advise evangelists to let it be understood by serious and good ministers that they sympathize with them and have no disposition whatever to disturb their relation or hinder them in their work, or crowd into their pulpits or among their people at the hazard of alienation and distraction rather than with the prospect of union and of gospel love. No other course can so readily secure the confidence of pastors. If pastors find that there is no danger that evangelists will break in upon their labors and disturb their relations they will invite them the more readily and cordially to come. If they find that an evangelist duly appreciates the pastoral relation, its difficulties and the danger of disturbing it—in short if they find that the evangelist most sincerely aims at promoting a healthful and stable pastoral influence—if they become satisfied that he truly aims at the glory of God and has correct views of the best means of securing this end, they will of course give him their confidence. If they love revivals and love the cause he loves, alienation will cease, and confidence be established.

I suppose it true, however, that under some circumstances it may be the duty of evangelists or other ministers to go into a region and there labor in the gospel, entirely regardless of the nominal ministry of that region. Where ministers are manifestly unconverted and churches apostate from God and spiritual desolation reigning, it may be and doubtless often is the duty of ministers to go and preach the gospel regardless of the nominal ministry there. But when the ministry are manifestly pious men and not opposed to revivals, their relation to the churches should be respected. If they have difficulties in respect to evangelists growing out of prejudice or misapprehension, let evangelists labor on where they have access to the churches until prejudice gives way and misapprehensions are corrected. Then a door may be opened to those fields where before only a small minority desired his labors.

Cases of this kind sometimes occur. A few zealous and perhaps furious men will insist upon the evangelist coming forthwith, and will write to him to this effect more or less fully representing to him, that their minister and the mass of the church are opposed to revivals. Now if he listens to such men, insists on his own prejudices, till he becomes excited, breaks in and goes to preaching before the way is prepared for him, the Lord will almost certainly rebuke him, and five years' time will show that his labors there resulted in more harm than good.

An able evangelist—one who is really discreet, simple-hearted and useful, will always find fields enough fully open for his labors. If he will be satisfied to follow the order of God and not suffer himself to be pulled or thrust in, before the way is prepared in the view of the pastor and church for him to come, he cannot fail ultimately to secure not only the co-operation of a pious ministry and church, but also to find access to as many pulpits as he can possibly occupy.

I have many things to say respecting the errors of evangelists, pastors, and churches on this subject, but let this suffice for the present.

Your brother,

C. G. Finney

March 18, 1846

Dear Brethren:

Although the employment of evangelists to promote revivals is manifestly in accordance with the order of God, and is of great service to the churches, yet I have observed that the churches are liable to fall, and in some instances have fallen into injurious errors in respect to their labors which have greatly hindered their usefulness, disheartened their pastors, and led them almost to the conclusion that upon the whole the labors of evangelists though in many cases immediately serviceable are ultimately the greater of two evils, or perhaps more strictly the less of two goods. Some of these evils which I have observed are the following.

The churches are liable to fall, and sometimes have fallen into the belief that they can have no revival at all without the labors of an evangelist, and they have had no faith or courage to make the requisite effort unless they could get some celebrated evangelist to aid their pastor. This belief wherever it prevails has a pernicious influence in a great many respects.

It leads the church in reality away from God to trust in man. Churches are not aware of this; but I have often seen so great evidence of it that I could not doubt it. During my own labors as an evangelist I have in several instances found the chief obstacles to success in the fact that the church were expecting that if I came they should have a revival of course. I have sometimes found it more difficult to convince the church of sin on this point than upon almost any other; and yet it has been impossible to promote a revival until they are convicted upon this point and deeply humbled and brought to see that they had been trusting in man rather than in God. When they had repented and put away this sin and looked alone to God in faith to pour out His Spirit, the work would revive and go on; but not before.

This is a much more common error than churches are aware of, and it is apt to prevail precisely in proportion to the known success that attends the labors of an evangelist. If his success has been uniform and great, the churches fall into the mistake of expecting as a matter of course that if they secure his labors they shall have a revival, and thus they dishonor God and seriously embarrass the evangelist.

But another aspect of this error is that church members throw aside personal responsibility in a great measure, and instead of feeling that they themselves must do a great part of the labor, under God, they often expect the evangelist and the pastor to do the labor, while they take a kind of passive attitude or at the utmost go into a kind of superficial excitement and bluster about to get people out to meeting and warn sinners as they express it, without breaking up their own fallow ground and getting into such deep sympathy with God as to be able to prevail daily and hourly with God in prayer.

The more I have seen of revivals, the more I am satisfied that one of the principal errors into which ministers and churches have fallen is that ministers attempt to do too much of the labor themselves and do not throw enough personal responsibility upon each member of the church. Whenever an attempt is made to promote a revival without securing in the outset a thorough reformation in the church, a deep and thorough breaking up of the fallow ground and a mighty taking hold of God in prayer, it will be found in the end that the revival, if there should seem to be one, will be very superficial, and will leave the church more hardened than ever. It is exceedingly injurious to churches to send off and get an evangelist to labor among them unless they intend to lay themselves individually upon the altar, to consecrate their whole being to God, and to enter so deeply into sympathy with Christ as to travel in birth for souls, until Christ be formed within them. Ordinarily, if the right course be taken, churches may have revivals of religion and powerful revivals too without any ministers at all. There are comparatively few churches in this country that do not comprise men of sufficient intelligence to teach the essential things of the gospel, to instruct enquirers, and lead them to Christ, if they were only in the right state of mind themselves. If the churches would only get into a revival spirit themselves, they could hardly help having revivals among the impenitent, even though they have no preacher at all. I could relate several instances in which powerful revivals have been promoted altogether by intelligent laymen and women, where no minister could be had, or at least where no minister had been employed. But where a church has a pious pastor, one who fears God and loves souls, if they will do their duty they will find that as a general thing they can have revivals and even powerful revivals without employing evangelists. When they can secure this result under their own efforts and those of their pastor, it is in general more healthful for the church, does more to strengthen the influence and promote the usefulness of the pastor and more closely cements together the pastor and his flock in mutual sympathy and confidence. It better promotes the growth in grace of both pastor and people. It gives the pastor greater influence in training the converts and in leading and edifying the church. In short in almost every way, where a powerful revival of religion can be secured by the church and their pastor, this is by far the most desirable course. Where evangelists are employed it should rather be to strengthen and encourage the pastor in his work than to throw him into the background, impair the confidence of his people in him, and cast discouragements in his way. If I mistake not in most instances where evangelists have promoted revivals in such a way as to weaken the influence of pious and faithful pastors and impair the confidence their people had in them, where the people have almost worshiped the evangelist, and have consequently thought less of their pastor than before, it will be found ultimately that the revival has very much unsettled the congregation and unhinged the most desirable influences that should promote religion among them. In many such instances the revival seems to produce more harm than good.

Now this result is often owing to the very injudicious conduct of the church. They do not take right views of the subject. They ascribe too much to evangelists and far too little to their pastor. By this I do not mean that so far as the pastor himself is concerned, he would care or need to care how little is ascribed to him. But the evil lies farther back. If the church take a wrong view of the subject the mischief that results falls on themselves. Losing their confidence in their pastor renders it impossible for him afterwards to do them the good it is in his heart to do, and which he otherwise might do. The pastor has been perhaps for several months preparing the way for a revival, and already the spirit of prayer breathes in many hearts, and a spirit of supplication is poured upon the inhabitants of Judah and Jerusalem. As soon as these appearances betoken the approach of a revival, instead of thanking God and taking courage, and laying hold upon God in mighty prayer, each member of the church taking his place, man, woman and child—instead of holding prayer meetings and moving in a body to promote a genuine revival, depending under God upon their pastor to do the preaching, they often just at this crisis take a course that is highly injurious. They make a move to get an evangelist; the pastor sees that they have not confidence that he can preach so as to promote a revival. He feels distressed. As things are situated he does not like to refuse lest they should fail to have a revival. The very fact of his refusing might prevent a revival, even though they might have had a powerful one if they had said nothing about an evangelist. He therefore consents; they send and get an evangelist and have a revival.

Now the church are very apt right here to grieve the Spirit of God by failing to give the glory to God and failing to ascribe to the ordinary means of grace that which really belongs to them. They do not seem to see that they grieve the heart of God by undervaluing the pastoral relation and pastoral labors.

But if, where the way is thoroughly prepared for a revival, the church and pastor with right views and motives can agree in calling in the labors of a judicious evangelist, and will take throughout a judicious course, great numbers may be induced to attend the meetings, and in many cases vastly more good can be secured through his labors than without them.

If the Lord permit I will endeavor in a future letter to show what I regard as a judicious course on the part of the church, the pastor, and the evangelist.

Your brother,

C. G. Finney

April 1, 1846

Dear Brethren:

In my last letter I dwelt on the errors into which the churches fall in regard to the employment of evangelists, and said that, the Lord willing, in a future number I would state what I regard as a judicious course to be pursued by a church, a pastor, and an evangelist.

In the first place I observe that nothing should be done that shall in any way relieve the church from a sense of their own personal and individual responsibility. I have always observed that where several ministers were present, employed in the promotion of revivals, so much ministerial labor is apt to do much more hurt than good. And I had much rather be entirely alone as a minister in the promotion of revivals, than to have so many ministers present as to take nearly all the active labor out of the hands of the church. When ministers are present, they are expected to take the lead in all the meetings; and if a sufficient number of them are present, they of course occupy all the time, lead in prayer and in conversation, and, in short, take the work so completely out of the hands of the laymen as to throw them very much into a passive attitude.

Now no person can read the Gospel with his eye on this fact, without perceiving that the primitive apostles and ministers, together with the Holy Ghost, threw a great portion of the labor of diffusing the Gospel and spreading religion, on the great mass of Christian men and women. We find that while all the apostles remained at Jerusalem, the lay members were dispersed all abroad through the persecutions that arose about Stephen, and went everywhere preaching the Gospel. Now for the health of the church it is indispensable that they should be actively and individually employed in promoting the cause of religion. The more labor can be thrown on them the better. The more they are put forward in holding prayer meetings, in personal conversation from house to house, and in every way except in public preaching, the more it is for the health of the church, and for the real interests of piety in any community.

I know that some have been afraid that in this way, laymen would get out of their place, become proud and interfere with the office of the ministry. But I beg leave to say to my brethren, that I do not think it best for ministers to attempt to be the keepers of the humility of the laymen. The true way to make Christians *humble* is to make them *holy*. The true way to make them holy, is to push them forward in doing all they can by their own active exertions to promote religion; and especially to press them into positions where they will be constrained to sympathize deeply with Christ in regard to the salvation of sinners. For this purpose, nothing is like personal, individual effort to save the souls of men. This work, in order to promote a healthful piety, must be thrown as much as possible into the hands of the church at large; leaving for the minister the oversight and superintendence of the whole movement, together with the work of publicly preaching the Gospel. Work the laymen as much as possible into conducting the anxious meeting, into conducting and managing the prayer meeting, the conference meeting, and indeed throw everything upon the laymen that they can do. I am convinced that this is altogether the best policy; and indeed the only wise policy in promoting revivals of religion. If the laymen are ignorant, let the minister instruct them. If he is afraid to trust them in the anxious room to give directions to the inquiring sinners, let him hold one or more meetings if need be, with the laymen of his church for the very purpose of teaching them how to proceed in conducting an inquiry meeting, and how to assist in its labors. Let the minister take pains at all times, both in and out of seasons of revivals, to give the laymen and women in his church, such instruction, that they will know what to do to promote a revival; and then in the name of the Lord, throw the responsibility on them. If he attempts to do all the labor, first his health will soon fail, and he will break down; and secondly, the work cannot be done in this way: for the Lord has said, "I will be inquired of by the house of Israel (and not merely by ministers), to do these things for them."

Then, in short, if the question of employing an evangelist comes up, it is wise in the church to raise the question and have it distinctly understood, that whether an evangelist is employed or not, the work is not to be taken out of their hands, nor anything done, that will in the least degree, relieve them from a personal and individual responsibility. Nay, if they employ an evangelist, one of their principal objects should be, that through his experience they may be set to work to the best advantage, and have the greatest possible amount of labor thrown on them. The experience of an able evangelist in respect to the employment of the lay members in the promotion of the work may be of very great service to the church. An evangelist that does not employ the laymen and women in the promotion of revivals, will by no means promote to any considerable extent their growth in grace. It is naturally impossible that they should grow in grace only as they are drawn into so deep a sympathy with Christ, as to engage in such personal and individual labors in the promotion of revivals, as shall make them strong in the Lord and in the power of his might.

Your brother,

C. G. Finney

Chapter VIII

THE PROPER RELATIONSHIP BETWEEN PASTORS AND EVANGELISTS

Dear Brethren:

Another thing which should be avoided in attempting to promote a revival of religion by calling in the labors of an evangelist is the disturbing of the pastoral relation, or doing anything to weaken pastoral influence. I have already intimated in a former letter that churches are apt to err on this subject, and to undervalue the labors of a pastor, and greatly to over-value the labors of an evangelist. Thus they wrong their pastor, grieve the Spirit of God, and render it difficult or impossible for the pastor afterwards to do them the good that is in his heart, and which he might otherwise do them. If the pastor is a pious man—and if he is not he should not be a pastor—and indeed let the pastor be what he will, great pains should be taken not to bring the pastoral relation into contempt, or in any way to lower in the estimation of the church its high and sacred importance. Therefore the church in employing an evangelist should not think of setting aside the labors of their pastor for the time being, but simply to call in one who has experience, and is filled with the Spirit of God to aid him in their efforts to save souls.

Again they should never suffer themselves to institute comparisons between evangelists and their pastor that shall lead them to undervalue their pastor, and to almost worship the evangelist; for if they do this they will surely grieve the Spirit of God.

The great thing to be observed is, to do nothing that shall grieve the tender Spirit of the blessed God. It very often happens when evangelists are employed, that some members of the church will have so little confidence in the pastor, and such an unreasonable degree of confidence in the evangelist, as to say and do things that will greatly distress, grieve and ultimately offend the more considerate part of the church. Such individuals become enthusiastic in their admiration of the evangelist, and just in proportion, cold and almost contemptuous in their opinions and sayings in regard to their pastor. This always works a great evil. They are ready to go the whole length of everything the evangelist says and does, and if their pastor and the more considerate members of the church see anything in the evangelist, the tendency of which they deem injurious, and which they attempt to correct, that class of the church to which I have just alluded, become offended, accuse the pastor of being envious or jealous of the influence of the evangelist, and their brethren who think with their pastor, of being opposed to the work, etc. There are a great many dangers in this neighborhood that need to be guarded against. Such members are not considerate as they ought to be. Through the influence of such persons great odium has been brought on the labors of the evangelist; and in many instances it has rendered it very difficult for pastors to see their way clear in inviting evangelists to labor with them. The indiscretion of the churches has been in many instances so great as to lead them to form an entirely wrong estimate of the comparative value of the labors of pastors and evangelists.

Churches should consider that the pastoral relation is one of the most important relations on the earth; and the more permanent it is, if the pastor be a man of God, and what a pastor should be, the better it is for the people. By this I do not mean that circumstances may not occur that will render it very beneficial for churches to change their pastors, and for pastors to change their field of labor; for such cases in fact often do occur; but this I mean, that so long as a pastor can maintain his hold on the great mass of his hearers, keep their attention, secure their attendance at meetings, and their confidence in him as a pastor, the longer he remains with them the better. The longer he remains, the better he knows their wants, their habits, their temperament and everything that a pastor needs to know, to be in the highest degree useful to them. But however judicious and able a pastor may be, the novelty of calling in an evangelist, his method of presenting truth, the new trains of thought that he may start, and multitudes of such like things may arise, and fix the attention of the congregation; and if in all respects a judicious course be pursued, immense good may be the result. But let the churches remember that the labors of the evangelist are to be enjoyed but for a little season; and that if they intend to secure the permanent influence of pastoral labor, they must as far as possible encourage and strengthen the hands of the pastor in taking a leading part in the work. They should not desire to have him thrown into the background, but have him preach, and, so far as his health and circumstances will admit, go forward and take a leading part in all the meetings. He should give out the appointments, and indeed should be encouraged by the church and by the evangelist to do all in every way that he can, to promote the work and secure the confidence and sympathy of all classes of the people. If this is not done, there is great danger of grieving at least a part of the church, of creating a party in the congregation who will think that the pastor is superseded in his labors, and rather held in contempt—and then the Spirit of God will be grieved. The church should be very careful not to complain to the evangelist of their pastor, and thus lay a temptation before him to undervalue the character or labors of the pastor—lest he should grieve the Spirit, and himself say things that will work great mischief. It is of great importance that the evangelist and pastor should be as nearly one as possible, and that the church should so regard them; that the pastor should manifest and have confidence in the evangelist, and the evangelist should have and manifest confidence in the pastor, that they should thoroughly sympathize and cooperate together. If this cannot be done, it is extremely difficult to secure a good result.

Again, the evangelist should not suffer himself to listen to the complaints of church members about their pastor. And if anything does come to his ears that is of sufficient importance to require attention, he should candidly converse with the pastor alone, and get his version of the subject, and never suffer his ears to be filled with complaints about the pastor without communing in a most fraternal manner with the pastor himself in relation to those things. They must preserve the unity of the spirit in the bond of peace; and if they cannot do this, evil instead of good will result in their attempt to cooperate.

Your brother,

C. G. Finney

May 27, 1846

Dear Brethren:

Another thing that should be noticed in this connection is the great temptation to which pastors and their particular and warm friends are exposed. If the Lord manifestly blesses the labors of the evangelist, Satan will not infrequently make powerful efforts to disturb and unsettle the confidence of the pastor, perhaps urging that he was never called to preach the gospel, that the Lord does not bless his labors and that he may as well retire from the ministry. Especially is he in danger of being attacked in this way if he has labored hard and long with little apparent success. If the blessing of God very manifestly attends the labors of the evangelist, it is very natural for Satan to take the advantage of him and of his particular friends, suggesting to him that his ministry is barren, that he is either not a Christian at all, or if he be a Christian that Christ has never called him to preach the gospel. Very much the same impression may be lodged in the minds of many of his particular friends.

Temptations of this kind often work great mischief in discouraging the pastor, in disheartening the church, begetting unbelief in both the pastor and his flock in respect to the progress of the work under the labors of the pastor. These discouraging suggestions are doubtless often intended by the adversary to prepare the way to bring on the church disastrous reaction whenever the evangelist leaves the grounds.

Now this is a device of Satan much more frequently practiced I apprehend than is generally supposed. Should inquiry be made it would, I have no doubt, be very frequently found to be true that the minds of both the pastor and the leading members of the church have received these impressions and suggestions from time to time during the progress of the work under the labors of the evangelist. And these impressions have been so often repeated on different minds that have had no communication with each other with respect to the subject, that a deep impression of discouragement has been lodged in their minds; so much so that the pastor has really very little courage and faith in attempting to carry on the work when the evangelist has gone; and the church have very little courage and faith to lay hold and sustain him.

In other circumstances it may be expected that Satan will take a different tack and ply both the pastor and the people, especially his particular friends, with another view of the subject. He will endeavor to stimulate a spirit of ambition and envy and jealousy in the mind of the pastor, and endeavor to make him unwilling to have the labors of the evangelist blessed in promoting religion in his congregation. And if there be any constitutional tendency in the pastor's mind to ambition, or in the mind of his wife, an hundred to one if Satan does not exert himself to overthrow them by attacking them in this particular manner. He will endeavor to excite in them the spirit of envy and jealousy in view of the fact that the people are becoming so much attached to the evangelist and so much under his influence. And right here he will often, if I am not mistaken, excite the members of the church to speak in the presence of the pastor and of his wife, in terms of great admiration of the evangelist, of his wisdom, talents and piety, and oftentimes put them up inconsiderately to say things that have a strong tendency to produce in the mind of the pastor and his wife just that state of mind at which he is aiming. His object is to destroy the spirituality, the piety and the usefulness of the pastor and his wife, to excite in them a spirit of ambition and jealousy so as to ruin their influence among the people. On the one hand he will make direct suggestions to them and on the other press the members of the church to make such remarks and to conduct themselves toward both the pastor and the evangelist in a manner that is calculated to accomplish his infernal design. What he aims to accomplish in the minds of the pastor and his wife, he will aim at bringing to pass in the minds of his particular friends in the church and congregation, exciting them to envy and jealousy and to resist the evangelist, because, as Satan makes them believe, through his influence their pastor is thrown into the background and his influence crippled.

It is sometimes very awesome to see in how many ways Satan will endeavor to bring about divisions and discord, to injure the influence both of the evangelist and of the pastor, if possible to create distrust and alienation between them; and if he cannot effect this, to create divisions in the church, so that one shall say, "I am of Paul, and another, I am of Apollos." The devices of Satan in these respects must be strongly and sedulously guarded against, or he will greatly embarrass the movements of an evangelist and greatly distract the church.

The more I have seen of the policy of Satan in this respect, the more I have appreciated the importance of the labors of evangelists, and also the great necessity of evangelists and pastors and churches being on their guard against an influence, which they do not suspect to be from Satan, being exerted not only to overthrow individual revivals, but to bring about a state of things that will cripple the general usefulness of evangelists and unite pastors and churches in resisting them.

Were it proper to enter into detail on such a subject as this, I think I might relate a great many facts that have come to my knowledge that would throw much light on this subject. Those who have labored much as evangelists must have had considerable experience in respect to the policy and movements of Satan in these matters.

I have thought for several years of inviting all the evangelists in this country to meet in a general conference and compare views, look over the field, pray and converse together with respect to what is to be done for the further extension of revivals of religion; and also of inviting to meet with them all those pastors who take an interest in the labors of evangelists, and who are anxious to prove all things and to hold fast that which is good, especially in respect to the promotion of revivals of religion.

Brethren, can we not have such a convention? Is it not time that evangelists and revival pastors have a protracted meeting among themselves, compare views, sympathize with each other, freely unbosom ourselves to one another, and devise ways and means of promoting and extending a revival influence throughout the world?

Your brother,

C. G. Finney

June 24, 1846

Dear Brethren:

One of the particular dangers of evangelists is that their labors may disturb the pastoral relations. This is not necessarily so, but such are the infirmities of human nature, and so many are the mistakes into which pastors, evangelists, and churches are liable to fall, that as a matter of fact the labors of evangelists have often tended strongly to this result; insomuch that churches have very often come to doubt the expediency, or to say the least, to feel very little of the necessity and importance of the pastoral relation. And this is a great evil. It has resulted in a great measure if I am not mistaken, from a fault in pastors and churches themselves, and doubtless in some instances from the faults of the evangelists. If pastors were really what they ought to be, it would be very difficult for the churches to be so beguiled by Satan as to come to think lightly of the importance of the pastoral relation. But where a pastor has been settled for years, and very little unction and effect have attended his preaching, few additions have been made to the church—all have slept and been quiet, until an evangelist comes forward anointed with the Holy Ghost and with power, and a great revival occurs under his preaching. In cases like this if churches are not strongly on their guard, these facts will lead them to take a superficial and even a totally erroneous view of the pastoral relation.

Now it is by no means justifiable in pastors to refuse evangelists because of the tendency of their labors to unsettle pastors in cases similar to that which I have just mentioned. They ought to be sensible that the fault may be and probably is in a great measure their own. The manifest barrenness and want of unction in their own minister is so strongly contrasted with the unction and power of the evangelist, that the inference is inevitable that their pastor is not such a minister as he ought to be.

And when they look abroad and see nearly all the pastors of their acquaintance in about the same state with their own pastor, they very naturally and almost inevitably infer that there is something in the relation of pastors which leads them to take matters easily, to live on their salaries, keep things quiet and build up their congregations, rather in worldliness than in the Holy Ghost and in faith.

And here I must remark again that in many instances it is the case that the labors of an evangelist are called for from the want of unction in a pastor. Now when this is the case, it tends greatly of necessity to injure the influence of the pastor and to cause the expectations of the people to set loosely upon him, and oftentimes results in destroying their confidence in him as a useful minister of the gospel.

Again it often happens that the evangelist himself will perceive and cannot but perceive that the difficulty is with the pastor—that he is worldly-minded and temporizing—that he has adopted a carnal policy—is seeking to promote this popularity, and many such things over which the evangelist cannot but secretly and deeply sorrow: In such cases he is often greatly at a loss—first, to know whether under the circumstances it is wise for him to go to labor with such a pastor—secondly, when he is with him, to know what course to take. He sees that the church has no confidence in its pastor and that it has no right to have. Perhaps the most spiritual members of the church venture to breathe to him their misgivings and trials of mind with respect to the spiritual state and influence of the pastor. In such cases it is extremely difficult often for the evangelist to approach the minister and read his heart on the subject of his spiritual state without giving offence. Indeed it is very difficult for an evangelist to labor extensively among those churches and pastors who are settled on their lees, without finding himself surrounded with accumulated difficulties. In spite of himself his labors if successful will naturally tend to make the churches see how far their pastors have been out of the way, and where the pastors do not come into such a state as to confess to their churches and reform their ministerial character and influence, the churches will in a great measure lose their confidence in the efficiency and usefulness of their pastor without any fault on the part of the evangelist, and secondly be led to undervalue the pastoral relation in general.

Here are many dangers and faults on all hands that ought to be looked at, realized, repented of and put away in order to secure the highest influence of both pastors and evangelists. The pastoral relation is certainly of priceless value. It is no less certain that the labors of evangelists are extensively owned and blessed of God, and it is just as evident that much wakefulness, prayer, and attention will be requisite to guard effectually against the dangers in which Satan is wont to involve churches, pastors and evangelists. A volume might be written upon this subject, but I can only suggest a few things in these brief letters.

Your brother,

C. G. Finney